D1171082

Praise for

THE
NEW
MOM
CODE

"One powerful book. Not just for new mothers, but for all mothers. The insights are profound. Amanda has the head of a brilliant analyst and the heart of all mothers who love their children to the moon and back. Reading this book will confirm your own insights and give words to the ones you have yet to express. This book is a keeper!"

—Dr. Nancy L. Stein, Professor Emeritus, Department of Psychology, PhD, University of Chicago

"Amanda's unique voice is the winning combination of a best new mom friend and the mom who unapologetically tells you how it is. In *The New Mom Code*, Amanda not only gives you the facts about postpartum life, but she also teaches you how to solve common problems in a fun, creative, and groundbreaking way. Get ready to fall in love with yourself again!"

—Christina Nicholson, TV Host, Founder of Podcast Clout, and Content Creator @ChristinaAllDay

"Motherhood can be so daunting and challenging at times, and yet we're not given the necessary information to conquer the ride before or after our babies are born. I loved reading Amanda's book; she gives helpful realistic advice for all moms for this new journey they're about to take and simple solutions to making #momlife easier and more rewarding."

—Robyn Lawley, Australian Supermodel, Mom, and Host of *Every Body* (exclusively on Audible)

"Every mom needs a relatable and blunt mom friend to talk about the truths of motherhood, but in a way that doesn't scare them. Amanda delivers in *The New Mom Code.* As someone who is working to normalize the necessity of infant sleep, I was happy to see Amanda share the importance of prioritizing rest and sleep for the entire family as an important ingredient in surviving the first years of motherhood."

—Ann Elaine Branca, Founder of Full Feedings and Other Ingredients for Infant Sleep

"In *The New Mom Code,* Amanda shares her stories of feeling completely lost in postpartum motherhood . . . and boy can I relate. She encourages us to search for who we are outside of the label Mom, who we want to be, and what lights us up in a time that can feel like exhausting and exciting daily explorations of new frontiers. In a time when it feels like everything has changed, our bodies included, we're allowed to feel wobbly while discovering who we are again."

—Emily Nolan, Host of *Brave Talks* and Founder of Topless Yoga

THE
NEW
MOM
CODE

Amanda Tice

THE
NEW
MOM
CODE

SHATTER EXPECTATIONS
AND CRUSH IT AT MOTHERHOOD

Published by Mandala Tree Press
www.mandalatreepress.com

Paperback ISBN: 9781954801288
Hardcover with Dust Jacket ISBN: 9781954801271
Case Laminate Hardcover ISBN: 9781954801332
eBook ISBN: 9781954801295

FAM032000 FAMILY & RELATIONSHIPS / Parenting / Motherhood
SEL016000 SELF-HELP / Personal Growth / Happiness
HEA024000 HEALTH & FITNESS / Women's Health

Cover design by Ashley Santoro
Edited by Melissa Miller
Typeset by Kaitlin Barwick

Cover photo by Emerson Miller
Interior photo by Tosca Radigonda

www.amandatice.com

I'd like to dedicate this book to my son,
George (who enlightens and delights me daily),
my husband, Peter (whose support and love
helped me to arrive here), my mother, Constance
(who has spent an endless amount of time and
effort teaching me almost everything I know),
and my father, Alan (who cultivated within me
the desire and value of helping others). Without
all your unconditional love, I don't know where
I'd be. I love you all to the moon and back!

Special thanks to Isaac Norbe, Alisa Guidette,
Josefin Adler, and Jennifer Hill for inspiring me
to keep writing, chugging along through the
publishing process, and chasing my lifelong dreams.

Contents

CONTENTS

Open your heart.
Welcome change.
Accept other mothers enduring the same.
Say goodbye to the past.
Join the village so vast.

Be your best self, no regrets.
Embrace your many assets.
You are resilient; you are bold.
It's time to break the mold.
It's time to rewrite the new mom code.

Introduction

Prior to having my son, George, I spent a lot of time in my underwear. In fact, I spent the last twelve years being a successful curve model for some of the most reputable and recognizable lingerie and swimwear companies in the world. That being said, my body looked and felt quite a bit different after I pushed out a seven-pound baby. Not only had I acquired countless skin tags and moles during my pregnancy, but I was also left with a variety pack of stretch marks along my abdomen. I should have expected this after gaining fifty pounds, but, alas, I was in denial about who I was about to become.

This became overwhelmingly apparent when my agent called and sent me to a last-minute request casting at fifteen weeks postpartum. Although it felt nice to have a reason to get dolled up for the first time in what felt like forever, I wasn't mentally or physically prepared for a swimwear casting. After arriving at the location, I waited thirty minutes before the client called my name and handed me a suit to try on. I struggled (and profusely sweated) in the changing stall as I squeezed my new body into a size 14 bikini.

The client then asked me to come out and take digitals as I quietly chuckled to myself in the mirror. It looked like I had two large watermelons perched on my chest, sandwiched together by one itty-bitty strap. I awkwardly exited the bathroom, doing my best to adjust every inch of the suit, which felt more like putting a rubber band around a water balloon. If I pulled up on the straps, I exposed under boob. If I pulled down on the straps, my nipples came dangerously close to popping out. And don't even get me started on the bottoms. When I tried to pull them up to cover my stretch marks, I was rewarded with camel toe and an uncomfortable wedgie. Then, when I pulled them down, realizing my bikini line wasn't well-shaved, it accentuated my "mommy top" (a.k.a., muffin top or tummy pooch).

The client politely took pictures of my front, side, and back and then thanked me for my time. As soon as I walked out of the office, I couldn't help but laugh. *Well, that was a nightmare*, I thought. *There's no way I'll be booking that job. And whose body was that in there anyway?* It didn't feel or look like mine. It felt like someone else's entirely!

Much to my surprise, two days later, my agent called to inform me that I had booked the job . . . and it wasn't just any job. It was for a television segment with Heidi Klum. I'd be showcasing her new swim line on *Access Hollywood*. I felt excited, horrified, and anxious simultaneously. I asked my agent if I could bring George on set to breastfeed as I thought maybe this would deter the client from still wanting to book me, but they graciously agreed. I had backed myself into a corner. I would be putting my postpartum body on display in a two-piece bikini on national television only sixteen weeks after giving birth.

Typically, the night before a job, I'd do my usual beauty routine: Take a long shower and deep condition my hair. Pluck my eyebrows, wax my lip, and then shave my arms, legs, and bikini line. Go to the salon to get a fresh manicure and pedicure. I'd pack my "modeling kit" with different types of bras, underwear, and high-quality hair extensions, all followed by eight or more solid hours of sleep. This had been my jam for over ten years, and I performed it regularly on autopilot . . . until the night before *this* job.

George was taking the four-month sleep regression very seriously, and my stress level was through the roof. I didn't have time to run out to a salon, so I attempted to clip and glue on fake nails while George napped (yep, they looked a hot mess). I couldn't focus on what I needed to bring for the job because I was concerned about what I might forget for George. Instead of searching for my magic strapless push-up and my seamless thongs, I meticulously searched and agonized over every item he might need in between breastfeeding sessions—diapers, wipes, disposable changing pads, rash cream, lovies, toys, extra clothes, a portable white noise machine, pacifiers, books, the works. I was a complete wreck.

Luckily, the actual job went relatively smooth despite my inner hysteria (and the fluctuating size of my breasts throughout the day). The client had allowed me to privately breastfeed George while he waited with my husband in between fittings and hair/makeup. Heidi was nice enough to take some selfies with me in the greenroom and show me what it meant to be a supermodel mom and mogul. She even gifted me the bikini after the shoot wrapped.

All that being said, the whole experience rocked me to the core. It was through that job that I realized I would never be my "old self" again—my priorities had shifted, and I had fundamentally changed. It made me feel deeply lost and confused standing next to the three other models on stage (all of whom were a decade younger than me). It made me ask myself, "How did I become someone so completely different in the span of a few months?" "How am I supposed to accept this new identity without *really* understanding it?" "Why wasn't I warned about this strange mid-life crisis feeling during any of my pre-birth classes?"

• • •

I think pre-motherhood, most women have an idealized fantasy of what their life might look like after giving birth. Maybe it's a baby that constantly coos and giggles; a toddler who always gives hugs, blows kisses, and says, "I wuv you"; a child who's brilliant, well-behaved, and caring; and a teen who somehow miraculously skips the rebellious stage. Maybe it's believing that you will be one of the lucky ones whose body miraculously bounces back within a matter of weeks. Maybe it's mistakenly thinking that you'll go back to work, and everything will be the same.

Somehow, pre-motherhood, most women gloss over some of the important realities that are heading their way at warp speed: bleeding and cracked nipples (so much fun, right? Ha!), endless laundry and meal planning, blow-out diapers and potty-training accidents, sleepless nights (and days), physical body changes (raise your hand if you wish you still had a strong bladder?!), ER and pediatrician visits, juggling more responsibilities than you ever thought possible, and so much more.

I also think that most women don't fully understand the magnitude of what happens when it comes down to the biological transformation that occurs during pregnancy as well as after birth . . . and the HORMONES. Holy mackerel. They are an unstoppable force of nature that induce unexplained crying spells, unexpected lash outs, and a plethora of other unsettling as well as euphoric emotions.

Now don't get your panties (or should I say hospital undies?) in a bunch about my brazen honesty. I'm just relaying to you how *my* journey into motherhood has been one big, fantastic, over-the-top, exhausting, and exhilarating rollercoaster ride thus far. In my opinion, being a mom is the absolute best job I've ever had (hands down) while simultaneously also being the hardest.

Let's be real here—motherhood is complicated, amazing, messy, exhausting, and blissful all at the same time. It's madness really. You give birth to the most spectacular child, whom you love more than anything in the world, and yet you're thrown into a cauldron of decisions, lessons, teachable moments, overwhelm, confusion, love, hope, and more. Your feelings about yourself change. Your feelings about family change. Your relationship with your partner changes. The way you live your life changes. As soon as your child is born, nothing will ever be the same, and that's beautiful, terrifying, intense, and dramatic.

This book is for all new (and new again) moms who have hit a wall and begun to ask themselves any or all of the following questions:

- Who am I now?
- What do I want for myself?
- Who do I want to be?
- How can I make the most of my child-free time?

For some mothers, it happens in the first few weeks or months postpartum. For others, it may not be until the moment you drop your child off at kindergarten and realize you have no clue what to do with yourself. Or this moment may not present itself until you've concluded that you're done having more children.

For me, the first time this feeling gut punched me was when I walked onto that *Access Hollywood* set. I felt like I didn't know who I was anymore. But after talking to a few of my closest mom friends, it became apparent that I wasn't the only one experiencing what seemed like a "mysterious phenomenon." Why hadn't anyone mentioned to me that I was going to be forced into a full mind, body, and soul makeover postpartum? Why hadn't any doctor or friend alerted me to the fact that there was an enormous physical and emotional obstacle course waiting for me at the end of pregnancy?

Truth is, there are a slew of commonalities between our unique experiences. It's just that someone, somewhere, at some point decided that certain norms should be secret (for no apparent or logical reason, that I can think of). And that sense of identity confusion you feel? It will continually fluctuate throughout your motherhood journey. There's no question that you'll feel differently when you have an infant, a kindergartener, and a teenager. The key to "rolling with the punches," however, is to validate, explore, and grow from each transformation.

When I made the conscious decision to write this book, my sole (or rather, soul) purpose was to help other mothers crawl through these pits of desperation and life-altering change. I knew that if I wrote this book, I could educate and support so many mothers on their journey to positively rediscover themselves, replenish their depleted stores, and help guide them to fall in love with the newest versions of themselves repeatedly (because operating on YOU 2.0, 3.0, or 4.0 is far superior to pre-baby YOU 1.0).

Mamas feel so much daily pressure that no one dares discuss. This book isn't about how to be a better parent; it's about how to tackle all the challenges you'll face now that you've become a mom. It's about saying the things that often go unsaid and acknowledging just how much moms endure without being awarded gold medals or Nobel prizes. It's not about what your new baby, toddler, or child is experiencing, but what *you* are. It's about rewiring how you perceive the "mommy culture" around you and acknowledging the past, embracing the future, and empowering you as a woman to be the best individual and mother you can be.

It all starts with reprogramming your internal code. Your "new mom code." What is the "new mom code" exactly? It is a new way of thinking about motherhood. It is a code that I have devised to help make your experience as a mother feel both guilt-free and inspired. It is a code meant to help you embrace the new person you have become and to give you the respect you rightfully deserve. It is meant to guide you through the various stages of self-transformation, including breastfeeding and burnout and preparation for the future. It's meant to help you shed your cocoon, become a butterfly, and learn to soar.

The new mom code requires that you actively set realistic expectations for yourself and accept as well as welcome the obstacles you will ultimately face as you make your way through your motherhood journey. This book will ask you to examine your current viewpoints and fiercely question them. It will involve polling your friends when you don't have the answers (even though it may be uncomfortable). It's all about being 100 percent honest with yourself and myth-busting "mommy norms" for you to break free from the damaging societal messages we unknowingly absorb. This book is for *you*, Mama.

I also felt compelled to write this book because I saw a true need for it when I suffered silently during the newborn phase. Although many of the books about motherhood and parenting on the market *do* provide lots of invaluable advice, they don't provide moms with practical, easy, quick, and tangible exercises they can do to change their behaviors and perspectives right now, in this very moment. Many things are often easier said (or read) than done. It's one thing to try and assimilate the information you're reading and it's another when you're asked to *do* an exercise that has the potential to spark immediate enlightenment. My sincere hope is that this book will provide you with the knowledge, tips, and tricks to feel like your best self, living your best life . . . because life is too short not to, don't you think?

I also want you to know that this book will only work for you if you're wholly honest with yourself and open to trying new things. If you want to crack the new mom code and break through to the other side (where I can guarantee there is a pot of emotional gold waiting), then you must put in the necessary time. But the great thing about this book is that you can revisit it whenever you please and complete the journal reflections and exercises at whatever pace feels right for you.

My hope is that this book will act as your personal cheerleader, giving you the insight and empowerment you need to jump over the daily hurdles that present themselves. This book is structured in bite-sized chunks so you can get the most out of your bathroom breaks and pumping sessions. You'll find that it flows like this: personal stories, useful advice, and journal prompts followed by a fun, easy, and powerful exercise.

I'm rooting for you. There's no question that you are amazing, so it's time to start recognizing just how incredible you really are. You've got this, Mama. I promise.

Please note: Throughout this book, I share personal stories from other mothers. Some of these mothers are friends of mine, while others are mothers who responded to questions in online groups. Most names and corresponding locations have been changed to protect their privacy.

Materials List

I believe as human beings we have an inherent desire to grow and change. Becoming a mother often brings up questions like

- Who was I before I had a baby?
- What is truly important to me now?
- Who do I want to be outside of "Mom"?

I have designed several exercises to help you reclaim yourself, gain emotional clarity, and more easily cope with these important life changes. These fun, easy, and positive exercises may be unconventional (and make you feel slightly squeamish), but that's all an important part of transformation. You will need all these materials in order to complete the exercises in this book:

- a journal
- a planner or a scheduling app
- 5 pieces of loose colored paper
- a washable marker
- thin and soft tipped pen
- body soap (any type will work)

- a camera or smart phone
- 10 pack of solid, lightly colored balloons
- one small pad of post-it notes
- a jar with a lid
- scissors

(Optional but highly recommended: safety pin, printer, individually wrapped pieces of dark chocolate, and extra pocket money you may have been saving for a rainy day)

May I Have a Quick Word?

Dear fellow Mom—

Before you embark upon this new and exciting journey, I need you to know something extremely important. I need you to know that I *see* you. I see you blearily waking up with your toddler's fingers on your eyelids and their little chunky legs straddling your disheveled, tired body. I see you making your coffee and their breakfast simultaneously while they climb the walls, slam the doors, and empty their toy bins. I see you struggling to get them dressed as you realize you are already late for an appointment, work, or school. I see your face as they dismantle the couch to jump on it, throwing the pillows and blankets all over the living room floor. I see you cleaning the milk/coffee/juice that they spilled all over the floor/bed/couch. I see you changing diapers anywhere and everywhere. I see you tolerating and enduring grocery/pharmacy/department store tantrums. I see you trying to keep the water in the tub as they thrash and splash around at bath time. I see you reading to them, cuddling them, and kissing them goodnight.

I *see* you . . . and you know what? You're a force of nature. You're Super Mom. You are the sun that lights up their entire world. We both know that you're doing *your* best. You should be extremely proud of yourself because you have taken on the incredible responsibility of teaching, caring, loving, and embracing a growing little human being (or clan, for that matter)! Mothers never get the credit they deserve . . . which is why I'm going to lead you down a path of meaningful and transformational self-discovery. I've got your back!

Xo, Amanda Tice

Chapter 1

WHAT THE HECK HAPPENED?!?

UNDERSTANDING THE SCIENCE BEHIND POSTPARTUM NORMS

"Being a mother is learning about strengths
you didn't know you had and dealing
with fears you didn't know existed."

Linda Wooten

The first day after my son's birth was somewhat of a blur, but I do remember a few things quite vividly. I remember how much it hurt to pee, the endless stream of blood that poured out of my nether regions, and how ridiculously bloated I still was. I hadn't anticipated that I would be holding ice packs on my crotch, squirting it with something called witch hazel multiple times a day, and wearing overnight pads (a.k.a., adult diapers) of my own. The pain and swelling were real, just as the love for this new little "bundle of joy" was real as well. Every time I looked at his face, I couldn't help but feel giddy and deeply in love. His tiny little lips, his long dark eyelashes, and his insanely soft hair were all incredibly intoxicating . . . and that smell. There is nothing like that newborn smell. My son, George, was perfect (just like all your babies and children are too).

For me, when I reflect on how I've changed since day one, the reality is glaringly different. My purse no longer carries lipstick and mints, but instead antibacterial wipes and healthy snacks. My wardrobe went from short shorts and the occasional crop to anything deemed yoga clothes (even though I'm rarely headed to a yoga class). My nights out used to consist of eating at swanky restaurants followed by drinks at trendy bars but were replaced with family-friendly restaurants with playscapes and kids' menus. My free time was spent relaxing, reading, and watching Netflix, and now it seems like there's no such thing as "free time"—it's called "paid time" (babysitter, daycare, school, or the guilt of asking friends or family to watch your little one(s)).

I had done my fair share of reading about pregnancy and parenthood as well as taken classes about breastfeeding, swaddling, burping, infant CPR, and so on. So it came as a bit of a surprise to me just how utterly unprepared I was for the reality of what it meant to be a mom. Why didn't anyone tell me that my life was going to be turned upside down and inside out? Why didn't anyone tell me that my boobs would sag, gray hairs would make themselves a staple on my head, or that my pre-baby body would in fact always be just that . . . my *pre*-baby body? And why on earth didn't any of my other friends with children warn me that breastfeeding was going to be *very* painful and difficult? WHY?! I was a tad bitter that none of this information flowed freely between expectant and new moms.

Prior to having a baby, most everyone spends all their time congratulating you, rubbing your belly, telling you how excited they are for you, but always conveniently leaving out the "Oh, boy, you're pregnant. Once that baby comes, you're going to feel exhausted, beaten down, and clueless about life in every way that you can possibly conceive of."

· · ·

I truly feel like the journey into motherhood is akin to molting. The moment a woman gives birth, she sheds her old skin, and she herself is reborn. Whether she feels prepared or not, the changes she ultimately navigates will force her to become someone new. Motherhood is a mixed bag of emotions, and there's no shortcut around those feelings.

Have you ever heard of the word *matrescence*? It's an entire anthropological movement explored in the early 1970s and has yet to command mainstream media attention! Dr. Arelie Athan, PhD, shares her working definition of matrescense as, "The process of becoming a mother, coined by Dana Raphael, PhD (1973), is a developmental passage where a woman transitions through pre-conception, pregnancy and birth, surrogacy or adoption, to the postnatal period and beyond. The exact length of matrescence is individual, recurs with each child, and may arguably last a lifetime! The scope of the changes encompasses multiple domains—bio, psycho, social, political, spiritual—and can be likened to the developmental push of adolescence."[1] It baffles me that I hadn't heard of matrescence until I began seriously researching postpartum motherhood. Why isn't matrescence discussed in textbooks and recognized by the Webster's dictionary? How has this idea of matrescence been buried and hidden throughout the twenty-first century?

It's upsetting to me that more mothers don't talk about this ongoing process. We have somehow been culturally brainwashed to believe that we should have all the answers and instinctively know what to do as mothers, partners, and individuals once a baby is born. Reality is moms are also human, and there is a serious learning curve involved with assuming so many new roles. We all have our strengths and weaknesses. Just because we became mothers (overnight, I might add) doesn't mean that we suddenly possess the wisdom of a shaman or uncover the true meaning of life. What it means is that by giving birth we have *mostly* unknowingly chosen to take on innumerous new, exciting, and overwhelming responsibilities without much direction, guidance, or support. Sure, some elements of motherhood we're equipped to handle, but others need finesse.

Think about it. If you were to start a new job, wouldn't the manager take the time to train you before putting you out on the front lines? Most likely, yes. Do you think they would expect you to know everything about the inner workings of their company as well as how to maximize profit and efficiency? Absolutely not. Most companies would

---

1. Aurelie Anthan, PhD, "What is Matrescence? My working definition," *Matrescence* (personal blog), accessed August 9, 2021, https://www.matrescence .com.

train you as well as put in the time and energy necessary to ensure that you perform your best for them. For some insane reason, however, mothers aren't universally provided with handbooks, classes, or trainings on how to be moms. We're just supposed to figure it out (and most of us suffer silently while we do).

This is where I feel I must step up, speak out, and hold your hand. You need to know that it's okay that you don't have all the answers and it's okay to have a million gazillion questions about how to raise a child, how to navigate new family dynamics, and how to prioritize your needs and aspirations. Trust me, no mother knows what they're doing immediately after giving birth. Not one.

It's also important to point out that motherhood will look and feel very differently to each individual mother. Almost *everything* you experience, feel, and believe is normal. Why? Because there is no such thing as normal! No mother has the exact same birth story, child, set of parents, upbringing, and so on. We all have uniquely individual experiences (even though we undergo similar situations and transitions), and it breaks my heart that so many mothers carry around unnecessary shame and fear because we're societally ill-educated on postpartum feelings and occurrences.

I wanted nothing more than to hug my friend Mary when she shared with me, "No one told me you won't necessarily love your child at first sight. It took me several weeks to bond with my son." How horrifying is it that she didn't know that many mothers feel the exact same way? These feelings of inadequacy and guilt are a product of our health-care system and our motherhood code being flawed. They're both broken, and it's about time that we fix them.

That being said, let's get to it. It's impossible to wake up in the morning after having a baby and not think, "What the heck just happened?!" Although I am not a board-certified physician, I feel, as your new mom friend, I owe it to you to share some of the transformations your body has endured and what exactly happens in the weeks and years following birth. This is real talk, mamas, no holds barred.

MOM BRAIN

Let's start by talking about "mom brain" or "mom fog" or more bluntly, what I would characterize more like . . . "Where on earth did I put my keys?" "What time was that pediatrician appointment on Thursday?" "Why am I getting so emotional all of the sudden?" "When did I become so absentminded and disorganized?"

Sue from Oregon shared, "Remember when your parents would call you by every name except yours? The dog, your sibling, their siblings? Well, that happens now! Also, I often forget to hit start on the Instant Pot because I'm just relieved that I'm about to get dinner on the table in a timely manner (or so I think!)."

Does that sound about right to you? Because it does to me, and there's no way that I'm blaming this kind of craziness on myself. It must be biological, and drumroll, please . . . it is.

According to an article published in *Scientific American*, "During pregnancy women undergo significant brain remodeling that persists for at least two years after birth. [There is also] preliminary evidence that this remodeling may play a role in helping women transition into motherhood."[2]

Basically, our brain physically changes during pregnancy in order to help ensure that we don't abandon our children in an alleyway once they're born. If certain structural changes did not occur, there would be a high likelihood that we might not endure the bouts of infant crying, the sleeplessness, and the complete overwhelm that proceed the first few months of parenthood.

More specifically, the actual gray matter of the brain, which controls social cognition and theory of mind, changes profoundly during pregnancy and there's absolutely *nothing* you can do about it.[3] As infuriating as having "mom brain" can be, Dr. Pilyoung Kim says that when a woman is pregnant "some parts of her brain actually *grow* [after she gives birth], specifically to support her new role as a parent. We observed significant structural growth in . . . the prefrontal cortex region, which is involved in decision-making, learning, and regulating our feelings and thoughts, over the first three to four months of motherhood."[4]

2. Catherine Caruso, "Pregnancy Causes Lasting Changes in a Woman's Brain," *Scientific American* (December 19, 2016), https://www.scientificamerican.com/article/pregnancy-causes-lasting-changes-in-a-womans-brain.

3. E. Hoekzema, E. Barba-Müller, C. Pozzobon, et al., "Pregnancy Leads to Long-Lasting Changes in Human Brain Structure," *Natural Neuroscience* 20 (February 2017): 287–96, https://doi.org/10.1038/nn.4458.

4. Katie Heaney, "What 'Mommy Brain' Really Looks Like," *New York* (The Cut), May 24, 2018, https://www.thecut.com/2018/05/science-of-brain-after-giving-birth.html.

She also goes on to say that "our brain probably does have a limit on how many resources it has. And for a few months after having a baby, the most important task for the mom is to take care of her baby. . . . A lot of her efforts and resources, and her brain's resources, go into that part of her life. So, you know, there might be some other things that she was really good at before that may not be at the same level for a while (like remembering things, for instance)."[5]

Does that make you feel any better? I hope so. Kathleen from Illinois put it best when she said, "I think there's an additional tax on my brain because of all of the responsibilities I have added! There's a whole new set of checklists all the time my brain is delivering on, all on inadequate sleep, in service of someone too little to even say thank you!"

So go ahead and tell your other mom friends that they're not crazy and that "mom brain" is a real, clinically proven condition that should be more widely discussed and accepted . . . and if your partner is giving you a hard time, go ahead and remind them that your brain is just in the process of miraculously growing so that you are a better mom. (Take that!)

HORMONAL CHANGES

Although I consciously know that hormones are present for a very good reason (that reason being having maternal instincts to choose the right partner and support our spawn), it doesn't negate that I also don't despise them. I don't know

---

5. Heaney, "What 'Mommy Brain' Really Looks Like."

any woman who looks down at a toilet full of blood and rejoices, "Yay! My period came!" (Unless, of course, you had been fretting about the possibility of an unexpected pregnancy, ha!) Yes, hormones are a natural part of life, but the monthly (or daily) emotional rollercoaster we are forced to endure as women is just plain cruel. It is only exacerbated during pregnancy and after birth. It is a miracle that *all* women don't completely lose it during the entire process.

According to psychologist Ann Dunnewold, "Right after giving birth, your estrogen and progesterone levels drop dramatically, which can contribute to 'baby blues' . . . or postpartum depression. . . . Meanwhile, oxytocin, which is called the 'bonding hormone,' floods your system right after delivery. . . . 'So, when oxytocin goes up, so can anxiety.' These hormones influence one another in a complex dance and affect your energy and mood."[6] It's safe to say that the fluctuation of these hormones is equivalent to someone pushing all of your emotional buttons simultaneously and hoping that you somehow survive. It's perfectly fair to say that these hormones are the reason that one moment you feel as high as a kite and the next you feel like jumping off a bridge.

Not only are your progesterone, estrogen, and oxytocin levels all over the map, but then you're also dealing with thyroid and relaxin hormones as well. These sets of hormones affect your body temperature, organ function, metabolism, joints, and bones. Therefore, now you're not only dealing with an emotional beast but a physical one too. Depending

---

6. Bonnie Schiedel, "17 Mind-Blowing Ways Your Body Changes after Giving Birth," *Today's Parent*, May 9, 2018, https://www.todaysparent.com/baby /postpartum-care/mind-blowing-ways-your-body-changes-after-giving-birth.

on myriad factors related to your birthing process (complications, genetic predispositions, length of labor, and so on), it's not unusual that you may also face extreme fatigue, rapid heartbeat, weight gain, dry skin, constipation, hair loss, joint pain—you name it. Christina from Florida said she was surprised to find out that her postpartum pain "wasn't from actually pushing the baby out—it was from hemorrhoids." You might as well be reading the fine print of potential side effects from a serious prescription narcotic.

Oh, and did I forget to mention that certain vitamins and minerals—like iron, for example—are sucked from your body? In terms of overall bodily damage, giving birth is the equivalent of losing a battle against Thor . . . but don't forget that it's a miracle, right? (There's no way on Earth that a man could tolerate giving birth. Us women have been given this "gift" for a reason.)

I don't know about you, but I needed to hear this. I felt like a complete basket case in the weeks leading up to George's birth as well as in the months (and years) afterward. I was quietly suffering thinking that there was something wrong with me instead of educating myself on pre- and postnatal norms.

I'm also an advocate of making the time to see a therapist or just having a good ole email or phone chat with your obstetrician. I'm sure either one could have helped to quell my gnawing anxiety. Resources are there for a reason and are meant to be utilized, so don't shy away from listening to your intuition. (And no, I don't mean going down the WebMD rabbit hole! You may stick your head down there looking for a nugget of useful advice only to suddenly emerge believing you have developed a rare and untreatable condition!)

BREASTFEEDING

Whoosh. Duh duh. Whoosh. Duh duh. Can you guess what sound I'm mimicking? Yep, you got it right. It's the sound of an automatic breast pump, a.k.a., a milking machine, extracting "liquid gold" from your sore and calloused nipples at *all* hours of the day. I swear my breast pump would whisper all kinds of strange and bizarre words to me over and over again at 2:00 a.m. It was more draining and exhausting than I ever thought possible, especially while also simultaneously trying to get George to latch by holding him in all sorts of weird and awkward positions. I tried everything my lactation consultant suggested, from nipple shields to emptying my breasts before feeding.

Even though I had read about breastfeeding and supposedly learned the appropriate special techniques through a class completely dedicated to the subject, no one seemed to address the important questions like, "What do I do when I'm engorged and my milk comes in?" (The answer: put warm compresses on your breasts or take a hot shower to encourage let down.) "How do you massage out a clogged milk duct?" (The answer: with difficulty, but your obstetrician can show you how.) "Can I get extremely ill from breastfeeding out of the blue?" (The answer: surprisingly, yes. Hello, mastitis.[7]) Breastfeeding is socially projected to be this supremely magical bonding experience whereby you give birth, and your baby simply and easily latches and then feeds on repeat.

Long story short, my personal experience with breastfeeding was far from magical. George latched for the first few days, and then I unknowingly became extremely engorged. Then, he stopped latching, and I exclusively pumped for over two and a half months before he suddenly decided he wanted to exclusively nurse and not take a bottle at all. It was grueling. The sterilizing, the filling and emptying of bottles and freezer bags, the scheduling and timing; it all tested my patience and my will. Whoever came up with the proverb "don't cry over spilled milk" obviously never breastfed! I was, however, thankful that he did decide to latch because, man oh man, nursing is much easier and cheaper than pumping or buying formula (which is *crazy* expensive). I was persistent in continuing my breastfeeding journey and weaned George at eighteen months.

Patrizia from Texas didn't have it easy with breastfeeding either: "When I was pregnant with my first baby, I was so excited about breastfeeding. I went to all the classes that the hospital provided and bought tons of stuff (covers, freezing bags, pump, etc.). When my son was finally born, it turned out that I had inverted nipples (which I didn't even know was

---

7. "Mastitis is an inflammation of the breast tissues that sometimes involves an infection. The inflammation results in breast pain, swelling, warmth, and redness. You might also have fever and chills," according to the Mayo Clinic, *Mastitis* (official website for the Mayo Clinic), accessed August 10, 2021, https://www.mayoclinic.org/diseases-conditions/mastitis/symptoms-causes/syc-20374829.

a thing), so he couldn't latch. Still, I tried with a shield. Days were passing, and my milk never came. Just a few drops here and there. I was so stubborn on my idea of breastfeeding that I kept trying and trying, and my poor baby was starving. The nurses at the hospital didn't help much either since they were pushing for breastfeeding too and were limiting formula. My baby cried the whole first night nonstop. Finally, thanks to my mom, we gave him a bottle. He chugged it in minutes, burped like an old man, and slept for eight hours. With my second one, I went straight to formula. Both of my kids are super healthy now."

Taryn from Washington had an entirely different problem: "Before I had my first, I was told by my allergist that breastfeeding was my only option. Formula was out of the question. My first had an undiagnosed lip tie, so I got mastitis thirteen times, and it sent me to the ER twice. Neither child would take a bottle, so pumping was not an option. I had to wait until nine months to try solid food, and it was a very slow and delayed introduction of solids in a certain order. I ended up breastfeeding for almost three years with each one. It all worked out, but it was a long and trying journey. The second one nursed naturally, which was a relief, but I still spent almost six straight years nursing."

The bottom line? *Fed is best.* Moms go through so much in those first few months of parenthood, and it's just downright unfair to judge a mom for whatever decision she chooses to make when it comes down to both her health and her baby's. A distraught overwhelmed mom = a distraught overwhelmed baby.

Now, let's get to the good stuff and touch on a few of the physical changes that your body endures when you're able to and choose to breastfeed. First, because of the drop in your estrogen and progesterone levels as well as the production of prolactin (the breast milk creation hormone), the size of your breasts will be in flux for as long as you continue to nurse. They'll most likely get bigger because of increased blood flow and milk production at the beginning of your breastfeeding journey, and then, once it ends, you'll end up with two flat flapjacks (a.k.a., two saggy, droopy, and misshapen breasts). I now understand why some women get implants after they have children. Those puppies are down for the count and won't stand up again without some surgical help or the world's best push-up bra.

On the upside, according to La Leche League (an international breastfeeding resource and support group), "During the postpartum period, breastfeeding resets the mother's metabolism to pre-pregnancy levels, and turns off the symptoms of metabolic syndrome. Otherwise, these symptoms continue into the postpartum period and beyond, eventually resulting in higher risk for diabetes and cardiovascular disease. . . . This is why you see significantly lower rates of diabetes and heart disease in older women who have breastfed for at least twelve months."[8] This equates to you not only burning an extra 200–500 calories per day,[9] but also decreasing

---

8. Kathleen Kendall-Tackett, "Breastfeeding: What's in It for Mothers?" *La Leche League International*, January 16, 2019, https://www.llli.org/whats-in-it-for-mothers.
9. Donna Murray, "Breastfeeding and the Calories You Eat," *Very Well Family*, accessed August 10, 2021, https://www.verywellfamily.com/how-many-extra-calories-does-a-breastfeeding-mom-need-431858.

your risk of developing certain diseases and conditions, including but not limited to breast and ovarian cancer.[10]

Breastfeeding from a biological standpoint is pretty amazing. If you've had the luxury of being able to do it for any duration of time, I hope you feel proud of your choice. Give yourself a pat on the back because it is insanely hard, and you deserve it. And if you chose formula, you deserve a pat on the back too! Fighting cultural pressure *and* spending every waking moment sterilizing bottles is equally taxing!

PHYSICAL CHANGES

In addition to the postpartum changes you may physically see in your breasts, a variety of other changes can occur too! Although all women have different bodily "reactions" to childbirth, many have similar experiences. The following is considered a list of normal changes:

- Your foot size may change due to the relaxin hormone.
- Your vagina will most likely widen.
- You may experience loss of bladder control and incontinence.
- You may need extra time to recover from an episiotomy (yeah, that's when a doctor makes a painful incision between the vaginal opening and the anus to provide baby with a spacious exit).

---

10. Erica H. Anstey, and Ginny Kincaid, "Breastfeeding for Cancer Prevention," Center for Disease Control (blog), accessed August 10, 2021, https://blogs.cdc .gov/cancer/2019/08/01/breastfeeding-for-cancer-prevention.

- You may lose a few teeth (eeek!).
- Stretch marks may find homes all over your body.
- You may have hair growth or loss for months.
- Your skin will likely change due to melanin (the pigment that adds color to your skin and hair), and you may also have hyperpigmentation, blotchy patches, and an abundance of skin tags.
- Your sex drive may take at least a year to recover, and your orgasms may be weaker.
- You may develop varicose veins and hemorrhoids.
- Your uterus may expand.
- You may experience a permanent abdominal separation (which creates a gap between your stomach muscles).
- Your hips may become permanently wider.[11]

So, yeah, that pre-baby body will in fact never be like your post-baby body, but that's okay! Don't forget that although you may have lost some bladder control, you gained a pretty freakin' awesome baby. As difficult as these changes may be to face, please know that they're all worth it. I promised you I'd educate you on these issues, and also that I'd give you tools and exercises in each chapter to help you move past the jarring nature of these newfound changes.

---

11. Laura Greggel, "18 ways pregnancy may change your body forever," *Live Science*, August 12, 2018, https://www.livescience.com/63291-post-pregnancy -changes.html.

Journal Reflection

It's time for your very first journal entry! Take five minutes and check in with yourself before putting pen to paper. Reflect on the changes you have endured since becoming a mother. What do you feel you have lost and gained? What have you learned about your body? About yourself? About family dynamics? Are you currently feeling weak or strong? Worried or confident? Why? Do your best to articulate what your motherhood journey has looked and felt like so far.

Exercise
EMBRACING THE NEW YOU

Materials: Journal, pen, and personal choice item
Time Commitment: 30 minutes
Cost: $10 and under

As a new mom, self-care and self-maintenance often falls to the bottom of the priority list. This shouldn't be the case, but it is typically the norm. Moms need as much care as babies and children do postpartum. Did you know that "about 70 to 80 percent of new mothers experience mood swings or negative feelings after giving birth"?[12] Between bodily changes, hormonal overload, pain, stress, and anxiety—it's time to acknowledge that these common

---

12. Valencia Higuera, "Recovery and Care after Delivery," Parenthood, Healthline, accessed August 10, 2021, https://www.healthline.com/health/postpartum-care.

postpartum conditions can't be ignored and moms need way more attention, support, and time for self-care than they're usually given.

An important part of self-care is learning how to love and respect your ever-changing postpartum body. Keep in mind that your body has performed a spectacular miracle and survived an internal battle. That's something to be infinitely proud of in and of itself! I like to call each new wrinkle, mole, incision, gray hair, or stretch mark a "mom gem" because they embody the physical representation of resilience and strength. I have enough "mom gems" to make an impressive collection at this point, and that's great because I love jewelry! The things that make you appear unique are in fact the most beautiful things you can wear.

SO, HERE WE GO!
HERE'S YOUR VERY FIRST EXERCISE!

Have you ever looked at someone else or in a magazine/on TV and thought, "Wow, I wish I could...?" These thoughts often come and go in superficial forms like... wear that lipstick shade, those jeans, my hair this or that way, and so on. So, the next question then becomes, *why* exactly can't you? You deserve to feel like the goddess that you are and embrace your newfound identity. You deserve to feel great in the new roles you've assumed and make time to take care of *you*. Be confident as you take on your new identity in this first activity: go shopping online or at one of your favorite stores and purchase something

($10 or less) that you want or have wanted to try but may have been out of your comfort zone before . . . and actually *try it out,* **today** (or when it arrives from Amazon, because, yes, I'm addicted to Amazon too).

FOLLOW-UP QUESTIONS

How did it make you feel to try something new that was out of your comfort zone? Will you do it again? Was it helpful to see yourself in a new light? Are there other things you might like to change, superficial or otherwise, that you feel are worth making time and space for?

Tice Advice:
EMBRACING CHANGE + SELF-CARE = LIBERATING, ENERGIZING, AND EMPOWERING THE NEW YOU.

"You are your own worst enemy. If you can learn to stop expecting impossible perfection, in yourself and others, you may find the happiness that has always eluded you."

Lisa Kleypas

Chapter 2
MOMBIE

How to Survive the Sleep Apocalypse

"When the going gets tough,
the tough take a nap."

Tom Hodgkinson

George definitely didn't choose "Mama" for his first word, or even his tenth. Before he said "Mombie," he said, "Dada, Doggie, Cheese, Shoes, Snack, Cracker"— you get the point. But, when he did say "Mombie," I was completely over the moon. He had hit the nail directly on the head. I was 100 percent his Mombie (Mom + Zombie = Mombie).

Before I had George, I loved to sleep. I mean, *really* loved to sleep. Anywhere. Everywhere. Any time of day and especially on any mode of transportation. (The white noise on an airplane . . . perfect for snoozin'.) All my close friends knew how much I loved my sleep and were afraid to warn me about just how little I'd be getting of it when George was born. Boy, was I in for it. The combination of sleeplessness and being strangely wired twenty-four hours a day during the newborn phase was brutal for me.

I did adhere to the "sleep when the baby sleeps" adage religiously. As soon as George would close his eyes, I'd lay down on the closest piece of furniture (or the floor), turn off my phone, and shut my eyes. I was desperate. I took every opportunity to sleep when George slept, for however long he would afford me the luxury.

The other well-known parenting tip "take turns with your partner during the night," however, my husband and I completely ignored (idiotically). Both my husband and I would wake up at all hours of the night together to soothe, feed, and change George. For the first three months, he fed George while I pumped. Neither of us got any decent sleep, or even a continuous five-hour stretch of sleep, until George was close to six months old.

I'd love to say it got much better from there, but it didn't. I chose to co-sleep, while my husband believed in using a traditional crib. He begrudgingly tolerated the co-sleeping until George's first birthday and then gave me an ultimatum. He told me if I wanted to sleep with George, that was my choice, but it was no longer his. Therefore, I could choose to sleep in our bed and put George in a crib, or I could choose to sleep with George (but not in our bed).

I knew this was fair, even though I wanted my way (of course). George wasn't a small baby (or toddler, for that matter), and he was (and continues to be) a complete wiggle worm. He kicks, he flails, he hugs, and he snuggles in the middle of the night. Keeping him still and calm was easier when I was breastfeeding, but as soon as I stopped, he became king of our king-sized bed at only 28 inches tall.

When that happened, I had no choice but to make a decision about our sleeping arrangements. What did I choose? I chose to sleep with George. That spurred a variety of bizarre and exhausting sleep routines that are only now beginning to be resolved almost four and a half years later.

Interested in what I tried? Here's a short list:

- George sleeping on my chest or directly next to me.
- George in a co-sleeping bassinet in between us in our bed.
- George in a crib in our bedroom, me in bed with my husband.
- George and I sleeping together in an "adult-sized crib" on the floor (a.k.a., a queen-sized air mattress surrounded by an enormous circular metal fence so that he couldn't crawl out).
- George and I sleeping in a queen-size bed together in a separate bedroom.
- George sleeping in a "big boy bed" (with a rail) in *his* bedroom, while I slept on the floor next to him (often holding his hand).
- George sleeping in his bed, while I slept in a kick-ass full-sized 20-inch tall, comfy blow-up mattress (with a memory foam topper) pushed next to his bed in his bedroom.

Yes, I tried "cry it out." Yes, I tried lovies, nightlights, blackout curtains, sound machines, special clocks, endless nighttime stories and podcasts, meditation tapes, melatonin, baths before bed—you name it. Yes, I absolutely lost my mind with our sleeping arrangements. No, it wasn't easy, and it exasperated my husband. No, despite all the crazy, he did not sleep through the night. He still woke up multiple times in the middle of the night (and continues to do so to this day!). I swear, I have tried it all.

Reality is, George just isn't a great sleeper. He is a little human, after all (with an abundance of energy and curiosity). The craziest part? Now that he has finally decided he wants to sleep in his own "big boy bed," in his own room, by himself (!!), I miss sleeping with him! He doesn't need me the way he used to anymore.

After four years of sleep craziness, I wouldn't really change a thing. They grow so fast, and those nighttime snuggles are always heavenly. So, be careful what you wish for, even if you are losing your ever-loving sanity. Your child will continue to grow and change every single day. That's a money-back guarantee that I can promise with utmost certainty.

. . .

I am not a sleep coach or a sleep expert. I am, in fact, the opposite. I would even go as far as to crown myself one of the world's most dysfunctional and erratic "sleep trainers." After George was born, all I wanted to do was to snuggle him, day and night. Feel his little head on my chest and his little fingers resting on my face. I was and continue to be a complete cuddle junkie.

I'm not going to give you *any* real sleep advice (because I don't have a clue about what I'm doing in that department), but what I *am* going to do is tell you that whatever you choose to do in the sleeping department is 100 percent okay. It's your family. It's your child. It's how *you* feel and what is right for *you*.

There is no "right" or normal sleeping arrangement in any part of the world. In Japan and India, it's common for families to co-sleep and is encouraged for as long as possible. In Latin America, mothers often choose to have their babies sleep in hammocks next to their beds. With the exception of making sure your child is safe at night (and doing whatever you can to prevent sudden infant death syndrome), pick whatever sleep situation makes you the *happiest*.

Want to sleep in bed with your child? Fantastic. Want them to sleep in a crib? Way to go! Want to sleep in their bedroom while your partner sleeps in the master? Not necessarily recommended, but hey, I'm not the only mother I know of who has made the same choice.

Here's the truth of the matter: more than a few of us are awful sleepers in this modern-day world (unless of course you've got a prescription for Ambien). Did you also know that "most of us experience mini-awakenings without even noticing them—up to twenty times per hour[?] When it comes to observable wakeups, most people have about two or three per night. But up to one in five Americans have difficulty getting back to sleep—a frustrating, sleep-robbing problem that experts call 'sleep maintenance insomnia.'"[13]

What does this mean for you? It means that you should do whatever you can to get some much-needed shut-eye. There's no need to feel sheepish telling your friends that you co-sleep or that you sleep in your child's room. If that's what works for you, then stick to it. Jessica from Texas told me that she sleeps with her husband, three children, and two Labradors in the same bed every night. And you know what? I commend her on choosing a solution that allows for her entire family to get the rest they all need.

Let me repeat (picture me holding a huge megaphone in front of my mouth): there's no one-size-fits-all solution when it comes to sleep. Monique from Delaware knew that she couldn't function at work without getting more Zs: "Returning to work after three months, I knew I had to figure out a game plan. I asked several friends what they did, and all of them said you have to do sleep training. It seemed impossible at first, but by night four it got so much easier." I applaud Monique on her determination to choose a plan, stick to it, and prioritize herself. Often, moms are so committed to taking care of their babies and children that they forget that they have basic needs too. Monique recognized this and took control of her situation.

April from Minnesota hit the nail on the head: "Sleep and mental health and general physical health are so deeply

---

13. "Up in the middle of the night? How to get back to sleep," John Hopkins Medicine (blog), accessed August 10, 2021, https://www .hopkinsmedicine.org/health/wellness-and-prevention/up-in-the-middle -of-the-night-how-to-get-back-to-sleep.

intertwined. It's so important to be rested, but it's also hard to give up the few hours of doing whatever I want between when baby goes to bed and when adults do. As a former night owl, it has been a big adjustment. But there's no substitute for a good night's sleep . . . I think I shaved some time off my life last year."

The best pseudo advice I can give, however, is for you to prioritize rest (in whatever capacity you can). If that means going to bed at 7:00 p.m., do it. If that means taking a fifteen-minute power nap during your lunch break at work, squeeze it in. If that means canceling plans or taking a sick day because you can't stand up straight, do whatever you can to take care of yourself. I'm giving you permission. Skip the laundry and lie down. Skip the dishes and take a long, hot bath. Please don't worry about household chores falling by the wayside or asking for help from your partner or a friend when you need it. A happy, well-rested mommy has a much greater positive impact on a family than clean stacks of folded laundry and dishes.

And hey, keep in mind that we're talking about scientific facts and fundamental biology here. Sleep is way more important than you may realize. It's seriously no joke, mamas. According to Dr. Harneet Walia, "A minimum of seven hours of sleep is a step in the right direction to improve your health."[14] But what if you let sleep take a back seat and

---

14. "Here's What Happens When You Don't Get Enough Sleep (and How Much You Really Need a Night): Sleep Needs by Age Group," Health Essentials, Cleveland Clinic, accessed August 10, 2021, https://health.clevelandclinic.org /happens-body-dont-get-enough-sleep.

keep cruising on much less than that? It may be a matter of life or death.

Here's a list of possible short-term problems associated with sleep deprivation (taken verbatim from the prestigious Cleveland Clinic):

1. **Lack of alertness**—Even missing as little as 1.5 hours can have an impact on how you feel.

2. **Excessive daytime sleepiness**—It can make you very sleepy and tired during the day.

3. **Impaired memory**—Lack of sleep can affect your ability to think, remember, and process information.

4. **Relationship stress**—It can make you feel moody, and you can become more likely to have conflicts with others.

5. **Quality of life**—You may become less likely to participate in normal daily activities or to exercise.

6. **Greater likelihood for car accidents**—Drowsy driving accounts for thousands of crashes, injuries, and fatalities each year, according to the National Highway Traffic Safety Administration.[15]

And what about the long-term effects?

"If you continue to operate without enough sleep, you may see more long-term and serious health problems. Some of the most serious potential problems associated with chronic sleep deprivation are high blood pressure, diabetes, heart attack, heart

---

15. "Here's What Happens When You Don't Get Enough Sleep," Health Essentials, Cleveland Clinic.

THE NEW MOM CODE

failure or stroke. Other potential problems include obesity, depression, impairment in immunity and lower sex drive.

"Chronic sleep deprivation can even affect your appearance. Over time, it can lead to premature wrinkling and dark circles under the eyes. There's also a link between lack of sleep and an increase in the stress hormone, cortisol, in the body. Cortisol can break down collagen, the protein that keeps skin smooth."[16]

I know it may seem impossible to cram seven hours of sleep a night into your daily schedule, but, Mama, you deserve it. You physically and emotionally need it. Your kids need you to have it . . . and my guess is that you prioritize their sleep, so why aren't you prioritizing your own? (I'm holding my picket sign high in the air and it reads, "MOMS DESERVE REST & RESPECT, NO MORE NEGLECT!")

---

16. "Here's What Happens When You Don't Get Enough Sleep," Health Essentials, Cleveland Clinic.

Journal Reflection

Are you content with your current sleeping arrangements? What, if anything, do you think you could do to improve your overall sleep quality? How does your partner feel about sleep? Are you on the same page? If not, do you see a reasonable compromise?

Exercise
TWEAK YOUR SCHEDULE

Materials: An online planning app or a weekly calendar
Time Commitment: 20 minutes (daily)
Budget: $0–$15 (depending on the planning tool you choose to purchase)

If you're still bleary-eyed and entrenched in the newborn stage, having a strict schedule will be almost impossible. However, once you pass about the two-month mark, people will begin to expect more from you (especially if you've gone back to work). With that being said, in this exercise, I'm going to ask you to schedule a short chunk of "Rest, Recuperation, and Recharge" (RRR) time for you to build into your daily and weekly routines. You must give precedence to RRR time as if it were a work meeting or an important appointment. What does this look like? Taking a power nap in the middle of the day on Tuesdays. Listening to a meditation tape or an uplifting podcast between phone calls on Wednesdays. Setting an alarm to make sure you're in bed by 9:00 p.m. on

Mondays and Thursdays. Choose whatever works best for your lifestyle, as long as you follow through, schedule it, and stick to it! Of course, you can move the timing around when things pop up, *but don't neglect it.* When you've got small children, you cannot put a price on sleep and rest. It's invaluable.

Also, let me reiterate that you *deserve* this time. Getting the sleep and RRR you need shouldn't be considered a luxury; it should be considered essential. And please make space to get seven or more hours of sleep at night! Don't forget what you just read about what happens when you don't. No feeling any mom guilt about this. As Eleanor Brownn says, "Rest and self-care are so important. When you take time to replenish your spirit, it allows you to serve others from the overflow. You cannot serve from an empty vessel."[17]

FOLLOW-UP QUESTIONS

After building RRR time into your daily schedule, how do you feel? Have you noticed any changes in your overall mood or demeanor? Have your sleeping arrangements improved or deteriorated? Why? Are you doing your best to get seven hours or more of sleep at night? Is there anything more you feel you'd like to try? If so, what's stopping you?

---

17. Eleanor Brownn, "Most Popular Quotes by Eleanor Brownn," *Eleanor Brownn* (blog), accessed August 10, 2021, http://www.eleanorbrownn.com.

(**Personal tip**: I am a Glenn Harrold Super Fan. His series of meditation tapes have saved me more than a few times and George even loves them too! ZZZZZ.)

Tice Advice:
BEFORE YOU WEEP,
TRY GETTING SOME SLEEP.

"There is a time for many words,
and there is also a time for sleep."

Homer, Philosopher

Chapter 3

JUMPING BACK IN THE SACK

RE-EVALUATING AND REINVENTING YOUR SEX LIFE

"Sex is an emotion in motion."

Mae West

It was my six-week postpartum checkup, and I was excited to show off George to my obstetrician. She was a fantastic doctor and held my hand (quite literally) throughout the entire pregnancy and delivery process. (She even left her Christmas vacation to make sure she was the one delivering my baby!) I couldn't wait to tell her everything about George and show her his big blue eyes and his precious teeny tiny fingers and toes.

I also knew this appointment was supposed to be all about *me* and *my* physical and mental health, but I couldn't help but glow with pride as she watched George quietly sleeping in his stroller. She asked me about my levels of anxiousness and stress, while also educating me about signs of postpartum depression. She wrote down a list of all the vitamins I was still taking, walked me through how to spot and remedy a clogged milk duct, and gave me exercises I could do in the event of sudden or mild incontinence.

Everything was going along just smoothly until . . . she asked me about sex and birth control. *Excuse me, what?! You have got to be kidding. You think I have sex on my mind? I can barely keep my eyes open, let alone consider mustering the energy to open my legs to do anything besides pee.* She gently reminded me that enough time had passed now that I could (1) become pregnant again (!!), and (2) my body had recovered *enough* that sex was back on the table.

Sex. All the sudden it came with a completely new meaning than it had before. No longer did I conjure up thoughts of making love or engaging in steamy trysts of animalistic desire. The idea of sex suddenly embodied the definition of actual baby making, and I sure as heck didn't want to risk getting pregnant again with a newborn at home.

On my drive back from the doctor's office, my mind began racing. Sex hadn't crossed my mind once since George had been born. Sure, I thought my husband was sexy, and he had been stepping up to the plate as a father, but I had zero physical or mental energy to even fathom the thought of doing it.

Then a slew of poignant questions bombarded my train of thought. Is my husband thinking about sex? Does he know that women can have sex again at six weeks postpartum? Does he know that we could get pregnant again right now if we aren't careful? Does he have a fresh box of condoms waiting for me in his medicine cabinet, or is he expecting me to start birth control again? And if it still hurts to wee, just how much is having sex going to hurt after pushing out a seven-pound baby?

As if I wasn't already consumed with adjusting to life with a newborn, I was now facing the fact that I might not be considering my husband's needs too. After that appointment, I realized that our sex life was going to take on a whole new life of its own; that sex was going to be and feel different and that I was going to need to start an open dialogue with my husband about our mutual needs and expectations.

· · ·

Okay, okay. I don't blame you if you're mad at me for being an advocate for your sex life right now. As Samantha from Connecticut put it, "I am always tired. For me, sex is a workout!" I know you're downright drained (no matter where you are in your parenthood journey), but I also know that some of the current issues you may be facing with or without your partner might be quickly remedied with a ramp up in romp sessions. No, I'm not asking you to join the mile-high club or order a swing on Amazon. What I'm trying to tell you is that sex matters a lot, probably more than you may realize. Just because you had a baby doesn't mean your sex life needs to die or that your partner has ceased to desire you.

It may take you four to nine months postpartum to pick up your stride (since it usually takes that long before you can get your baby into a reasonable sleep routine), but after that, it's time to prepare yourself to tango again . . . and again. Believe it or not, *you* need the intimate adult connection as much as your partner does.

Laura from Tennessee shared, "I was worried about how unsexy my new incision scar looked from having a c-section, and how huge my boobs were from my endless battle of unsuccessful breastfeeding, but my advice is to go on a date night, stop internalizing, and just have fun with your spouse! You are both different now in certain ways, but it's important to appreciate the change and get connected to each other."

I'm well aware that I'm not a sex therapist, but the research behind what I'm saying is compelling. Let's delve into what you may be experiencing now and what you might expect your sex life to look like a few years down the road.

THE FIRST 4-9 MONTHS

After all the extreme changes to your body and your lifestyle, it's no surprise that sex may fall to the bottom of your to-do list. Between raging hormones, lingering delivery pain, and having a tiny human glued to you twenty-four hours a day, sex may feel like an impossible feat. You may also be experiencing night sweats, vaginal dryness, and body dysmorphia as well as the baby blues.

On top of that, according to Dr. Rebecca Booth, "Nursing releases oxytocin, a hormone that triggers good feelings toward the baby but also suppresses your libido. Anthropologically speaking, keeping your sex drive low is your body's way of preventing another pregnancy too soon. Patients are always relieved to find out there's a reason they're not as into sex."[18]

Even though you may not be in the mood, the good news is that "giving birth awakens us to a range of sensations, and as a result, our bodies, particularly our genitals, become more alive, increasing our pleasure potential," says sex coach Amy Levine.[19] Yes, there's a good chance that the first time you have sex postpartum will hurt, but it will only be a matter of time before you get back into a comfortable and pain-free rhythm. As Eleanor from Florida put it, "I was very anxious to have sex after giving birth, but lube became my best friend during that time."

9-18 MONTHS

Although any time away from your child may still be very limited, nine to eighteen months is when things can get more interesting. No, I'm not asking you to bust out fuzzy handcuffs or buy a bunch of sex toys (unless you feel so inclined). What I'm telling you is that you're going to have to get a bit more creative about when and where you have sex. This is where carpeted floors and "nooners" become your friend. This is when quickies are actually quick, and the bedroom is actually used for sleeping. Anna from California shared,

---

18. Erin Zammett Ruddy, "8 Surprising Truths about Sex after Birth," *Parents Magazine*, updated April 12, 2021, accessed August 10, 2021, https://www.parents.com/parenting/relationships/sex-and-marriage-after-baby/how-to-have-great-postpartum-sex.
19. Ruddy, "8 Surprising Truths about Sex after Birth."

"We have sex in the tub or the guest bed after we put our son down, with the monitor beside us . . . and we just laugh about it when it turns into 'sexus interruptis.'"

It is also during this postpartum phase that you may have to reacquaint yourself with your partner in order to reconnect in completely new ways. "Intimate contact can come in many forms. Think in terms of sensual contact, sensual relaxation and sex play. . . . Do things you both genuinely enjoy that have some kind of physical component rather than being intercourse—and orgasm—focused," advises sex therapist Lisa Terrell.[20] This is the time when you get to explore a bit more of your new body, new roles, and new turn-ons. I honestly can't get enough of watching my husband mow the lawn on a hot summer day or successfully fix a leak under the kitchen sink (oh baby, oh baby, yeah!).

I think the key here is to really start playing with your partner again. No, the duration and frequency of sex will likely not return to the way it was pre-baby, but it has the potential to become way more fun and even more satisfying.

18 Months and Beyond

Once you're finally able to leave your child with a sitter, friend, or family member, that's when it's really important to kick it up a notch. As your life gets busy and you begin to resume a more regular schedule, that's when it's time

---

20. Erin van Vuuren, "Revving Up Your Sex Life After Baby: 7 Tips from the Pros," The Bump, updated August 6, 2020, https://www.thebump.com/a /revving-up-your-sex-life-after-baby.

to make sure you've pushed intimacy closer to the top of your to-do list. Clinical psychologist David Ley, PhD, says, "Having sex regularly has been linked to several health benefits, like feeling happier and even living longer."[21] When you take the time to connect with your partner through sex, studies show that your sleep and stress levels improve, and your relationship satisfaction elevates by opening up different channels of communication.[22] Sex begets more sex, and pleasure begets more pleasure. The more open you become with your partner, the stronger the bond you form with them.

It's also important to note that you will surely go through dry spells (everyone does), and you'll have periods of time when you and your partner can't seem to connect. But actively making the effort to keep that from happening will always be in your best interest. It's not so much about the frequency as it is about the quality. When you prioritize being on the same wavelength and operating at the same frequency, it's more likely that you both will feel like you can conquer the world together as individuals, partners, and parents. Heck, it wasn't until recently that I deeply understood just how paramount sexually connecting with my husband is to surviving the emotional rollercoaster that is parenthood.

---

21. Korin Miller, "This Is How Often Happy Couples Are Having Sex, According to Therapists," *Prevention Magazine*, June 14, 2019, https://www .prevention.com/sex/relationships/a24846275/how-often-do-couples-have-sex.
22. Miller, "This Is How Often Happy Couples Are Having Sex."

YOUR POSTPARTUM BODY

I know your body looks and feels a bit foreign right now, but please, *please* embrace it. Your body is freakin' incredible—it grew and birthed a tiny human! Remember how I talked about my "mom gems" in chapter one? I highly recommend that you adopt this phrase and urge yourself to take it seriously. It's completely unrealistic to expect that your body will look the same after giving birth. Learning to accept certain changes is important for your mental health. It makes me want to scream when new moms put an insane amount of pressure on themselves to "get their bodies back." If you were to get your old body back, you wouldn't have a baby, would you?

The media is partly to blame for why so many new mothers feel the need to lose weight and buy products to achieve certain goals, but you have the power to give all these magazines, television shows, social media, and news outlets the finger. Clinical therapist and eating-disorder recovery center founder Kyla Fox explained, "Women talk about the pressures they feel to diet immediately after giving birth, not realizing that cutting calories may compromise their ability to produce the milk required to feed their babies. Balanced nutrition and regulated intake are also critical for mental and emotional stability. Women tell me about the ways they are exercising to the point of exhaustion or going to the gym well before their doctor said it was safe. Our bodies need time to heal." She also went on to delightfully state, "Perhaps if we spent more time celebrating the women, and the incredible bodies that led to motherhood, we would be less inclined to celebrate them vanishing. Perhaps we could love those bodies. Perhaps we could even call them beautiful—*now* and always."[23] Perhaps you can be part of the movement to change the narrative. You have the power to decide. At the very least, I'm begging you to give your new body the love and confidence it craves, because, Mama, your body is magical and sexy—just the way it is!

BIRTH CONTROL

I don't know about you, but the idea of getting pregnant with a newborn in tow sounded bone-shatteringly exhausting and terrifying to me. This, my friend, is why it's necessary to seek out birth control at your six-week checkup. I mean, can you even imagine having morning sickness and breastfeeding simultaneously? Taking care of two babies only mere months apart in age? Having a toddler who's running and another baby crawling in opposite directions without fluid language skills yet? (Parents of twins, you are my heroes!)

Eeeek, it sounds all kinds of rough to me. So if it isn't in your family's plan to get pregnant again right away, make sure you are taking all the necessary precautions. Want to opt out of birth control for a while and go the condom route? Great! Want to put in an intrauterine device (IUD) so you don't have to think about it? Fantastic! Want your partner to

---

23. Kyla Fox, "Why You Shouldn't Try to Get Your Pre-Baby Body Back," *Today's Parent*, August 2, 2020, https://www.todaysparent.com/family/womens -health/why-you-shouldnt-try-to-get-your-pre-baby-body-back.

get snipped or have your tubes tied? Ah-mazing! If possible, research your options prior to your appointment and consult your OB on what she (or he) thinks is right for you. Just do yourself a favor and don't delay your plan of action once you decide to reignite your sex life or else you may end up with a very big unplanned oopsie.

Journal Reflection

How do you currently feel about sex or self-stimulation? Does it feel daunting, exciting, exhausting—a combination of the three? How are you feeling about your body? How do you feel your relationship with your partner has changed since giving birth? Are you getting the intimacy you feel you need? Do you think your partner's needs are being met? Do you want to make more time to have sex or pleasure yourself? If so, can you see a solution for making that happen?

Exercise
GET BACK IN THE SADDLE

Materials: Your partner, your hand, or your favorite sex toy
Time Commitment: 15 minutes
Budget: Free (or with the help of a paid sitter)

I'm sure you expected that the exercise in this chapter would involve sex, and surprise, surprise, of course it does! Although you may have been putting it off, it's time to take it off and go at it with your partner or dig out your vibrator. As long as you're six-weeks postpartum and your OB has given you the okay to play, it's time to rediscover your body with or without a partner. Whether you're attached or single, we all need stress relief. Making time for pleasure is the treasure you deserve. It might be awkward now. It will probably hurt (a lot). It might be mind-blowing. Or it might be a complete disaster. Regardless, you won't know until you try and keep trying (lots of different positions or toys). So, if necessary, schedule a date and time to make it happen, bust out the candles and Marvin Gaye, or corner your partner in the shower when your child is sleeping.

FOLLOW-UP QUESTIONS

Attached: How did it feel to have sex with your partner again? Do you feel a renewed sense of connection, or do you feel more deflated? How much sex do you think you both need right now? Would increasing the frequency help to alleviate certain stresses you're facing? How can you make the sex you are having more enjoyable or exhilarating?

Single: How did it feel to explore your body postpartum? Did you take the initiative to try something new or different? If so, do you think you might want to incorporate it into your routine? How do you think you could make your "stress relief time" even more enjoyable?

Tice Advice:
YOU MIGHT HAVE NINETY-NINE PROBLEMS,
BUT SEX DOESN'T NEED TO BE ONE.

"We are all born sexual creatures, thank God,
but it's a pity so many people despise
and crush this natural gift."

Marilyn Monroe

Chapter 4

FIND YOUR TRIBE, FIND YOUR VIBE

MASTERING THE ART OF MAKING MOM FRIENDS

"We all need a friend who understands
what we're not saying."

Unknown

When I was twenty-five weeks pregnant, I followed the advice of my OB and decided to sign up for a prenatal yoga class (even though I had never done yoga a day in my life). I told myself that I owed it to my growing baby to be the healthiest I could be. So when I arrived at my first class, I made all the first-time yoga rookie mistakes. I wore socks *and* shoes. I didn't have my own mat. I pushed and contorted my body in ways that it wasn't supposed to go (causing pain instead of relief). But despite my first-timer mishaps, I continued going twice a week, much to my own chagrin. Thank goodness I did.

By the time I was thirty weeks pregnant, yoga class had become part of my weekly routine, and I began to recognize all the names and faces of the women in the class. We all had to go around in a circle and introduce ourselves to the group by stating our names, how far along we were, whether we had determined names for our future child(ren), at what hospital we'd be delivering our babies, and so on and so forth. Having this little support group was quite informative and useful even though it meant that I had to "flow" through multiple positions I didn't particularly care for (like downward dog and tree pose).

I did, however, genuinely appreciate the social education I was getting through the class. But it wasn't until one morning when I was thirty-one weeks along that my life drastically changed. A young, gorgeous, bubbly white-blonde woman walked through the doors and squarely placed herself on her mat next to me. She was what Barbie dreams are made of, and I was in complete awe. She was wearing a hot-pink ensemble with matching pink socks. Her mat was magenta, and her water bottle was rose gold. She sheepishly looked around and then quietly introduced herself to me in a foreign accent, laughing a bit nervously at the entire setup. (It *is* pretty entertaining being in a room full of pregnant ladies with different sized and shaped bumps!) Her due date was two weeks before mine, and she had decided to begin yoga for all the same reasons I had.

As soon as class was over, I immediately asked for her number and set up our first "date." I knew from the moment I met her that she was one of a kind. She was the expectant mom friend I needed in my life and the one who would ultimately embark upon this motherhood journey with me. We had more in common than I ever could have hoped for, and she has turned out to be one of my very closest and most beloved friends.

. . .

If there's one thing I've learned about people, it's that they like to put each other into a variety of categories. They compartmentalize their relationships based on several factors, from instant connection to geographical convenience to disposition. I would say the most common categories people filter their relationships into are best friends, harmless peripheral distractions, and mortal enemies. Even though it's completely normal to categorize and sort relationships, I do find that most people tend to judge a book by its cover a bit too quickly. I think most of us would like to believe we're very good judges of character, but sadly, we're mistaken more often than not. We miss out on beautiful connections and deep friendships because we're scared. Scared to be hurt. Scared to be wrong. Scared of people who are wholly different from us. Scared to honestly speak our minds . . . and it's all absolutely ridiculous.

What do you think would happen if you stopped putting limitations on the type of relationship you could have with each person you encounter? Is it possible that your mortal enemy may need you or vice versa? Or that if you gave one of your peripheral distraction friends or convenience friends the time of day, they might end up being more reliable and supportive than your new "best friends"?

When you become a mom, the glaring reality is that you need a tribe. There's a reason why the saying "it takes a village to raise a child" is still widely used and disseminated. It's because you *do* need real support and honest feedback, especially from other new *and* seasoned moms. If you think you can do it without help from friends and family, I wish you the best but it's surely going to be a quick and easy path to misery, loneliness, depression, and desperation.

Truthfully, I don't know if I could have survived the first few months postpartum without Gwen (my prenatal yoga mom friend). During the first year, we compared endless notes a la . . . Is your child teething yet? Has your child ever gotten this type of rash or cough? Are they still crawling or are they walking? What diapers and diaper cream work best for you? When are you going to start solid foods? How and when will you wean? The Q&A text chats between us meant *everything* to me, especially when I didn't have the energy to pick up a book and try to figure out the answers myself.

We also cried on each other's shoulders (literally) and commiserated with each other about the changes in our bodies, lives, careers, and relationships. We shared all our daily minutia, which helped to alleviate the loneliness and isolation I felt after having a newborn and when leaving the house felt like an impossible feat (because, like . . . germs are *everywhere*. Lurking in every crevice and dark corner, and on countertops, doorknobs, and so on).

Don't get me wrong, as much as I shared so many of my daily experiences with Gwen, my other new mom friends were equally important. Even if I wasn't texting them daily or seeing them as often, their unique perspectives were very helpful. And let me tell you, it's always nice to take a little poll between friends when you're trying to make hundreds of mini decisions about the well-being of your child every single day.

I also think it's easy to forget sometimes that different people have different strengths. It's in your best interest to have a variety of mom friends because they each have something special to offer. For example, I have one friend who is a Pinterest master, another who shares simple healthy meal ideas on group chats, and another who is a doctor (who thankfully often answers any medical questions I have at 3:00 a.m.).

I have older and younger mom friends. I have mom friends with modernist, alternative, and stark traditionalist viewpoints. I have mom friends who have one child and others who have five. I have mom friends who lead a vegan lifestyle and others who wouldn't dare . . . and the truth is, each one of their perspectives is valuable to me. Each perspective helps me, as a mother, to decide which aspects of my parenting style are important to me and why. They each play an integral role in helping me make the best decisions I can for my family and myself. Isn't that what friends are for? Support and guidance? People who help carry you through storms and lift you up when you succeed? Believe me, when it comes to mom friends, your mantra should be, "The more the merrier," my friend. "The more the merrier." Repeat that one more time.

I also want to remind you how amazing it is to be open about letting new and diverse types of people into your life. You might be thoroughly surprised to find that they'll show up for you when you least expect it or teach you something you needed to learn. I can honestly say that I still make new mom friends every few months. Friends do come and go, but that's okay. Not everyone has to be your best friend for life. I believe you make certain friends for a reason or for a season, but each relationship has the capability of transforming and/or enriching your life.

Once you come to the realization that making new mom friends and finding a solid mom tribe should be on your to-do list, the next question will undoubtedly be, "But how do I do it?" Honestly, it's not always easy and it does require a certain amount of assertiveness. Here are some of the ways I have met some amazingly inspiring and remarkable moms:

CLASSES

I know, I know. I'm sure when you finished school, you didn't assume you'd be back taking classes again before you knew it, but here you are! Classes are the most obvious choice for meeting expectant and new moms, and there's a reason for that—they're usually the easiest and quickest way to meet the right moms at the right time. Want to meet an expectant mom who's twenty-five weeks pregnant? Go to a prenatal yoga class or infant CPR. Want to meet an expectant mom who's thirty-five-plus weeks pregnant? Go to a breastfeeding/swaddling/newborn prep class. Want to meet a new mom with a newborn? Go to a Mommy and Me class that is age specific, like Gymboree.

Although classes come with a cost, they are usually worth it. Even though I may not remember a single pose from my prenatal yoga class, I gained a loving, supportive, and invaluable group of mom friends who are still very much a part of my life (even though I now live halfway across the country). I highly recommend making these connections before you give birth, since then you aren't coping with all the newborn challenges alone. However, if you're struggling to make friends postpartum, then please consider other types of classes for your child: swimming, gymnastics, art, music, dance, and so on are all wonderful for toddlers and young children, not to mention they provide fantastic environments in which to connect and engage with other moms who have children of similar age. Brooke from Hawaii shared, "I have made mom friends through my kids' daycare. In fact, my four-year-old's entire class joined the same soccer team this past spring!"

GROUPS

Cliché, yes. Necessary, yes. Infinitely helpful, yes.

As much as Facebook has its pitfalls, it does have one major strength . . . groups. A quick search can seamlessly connect you with moms in your neighborhood and community. There are groups for first-time moms, local moms, mom meet-ups, mom support, sober moms, breast-feeding moms, older moms—almost anything you can imagine. I think it's best to initially join at least half a dozen. It's likely that you won't get everything you need from one group. Repeat after me, "The more the merrier." Each group has the ability to provide a different resource. Why not take advantage of free advice and support?

Meetup.com is also a great place to search for local mom playgroups. Often, the coordinator of these groups has connections at local libraries, museums, and book-stores. They also tend to set up meetings at parks, play-grounds, and kid-friendly restaurants. You need all of this, especially if you're a stay-at-home mom. Fresh air. New environments. A moment to breathe. I swear the days with babies and toddlers are more than twenty-four hours long (right?!), which means having scheduled activities is imper-ative to your survival and mental health. Without a rough routine and some advance planning, it's just a matter of time before overwhelm will set in. I know it takes effort and can be a bit of a pain, but a few fun and simple outings with mom friends can be a true lifesaver.

Kristy from California shared, "I met my first mom friend at a MOPS (Mothers of Preschoolers) meeting. I wasn't even sure what that was but desperately wanted some mommy friends and someone suggested it. So glad I did. I made friends with moms there that I still talk to nine years later. It was really great to have the support that came with MOPS."

Just like MOPS, the group "Moms Club" also has local chapters all over the country. Moms Club puts together fantastic activities, community service projects, and parties aimed at giving moms the opportunity to connect to one another with kiddos in tow. In smaller communities, Moms Club is amazing because moms take turns hosting events at their homes instead of at large, sometimes overpriced venues. These more intimate settings allow for a more relaxed environment for moms to really connect (unless, of course you're the one hosting that day! LOL!).

Want to shed some postpartum pounds and move your body? Fit4Mom also has local chapters all around the country and is a great way to find a local tribe. From Stroller Strides to Stroller Barre, you're sure to make new mom friends and improve your health at the same time. I even met one of my very best friends at the childcare check-in desk at my local gym.

It may seem daunting at first to join online or offline groups, but I promise you that it will make a world of difference in your level of saneness. Also, please don't get discouraged if the first sets of groups you join aren't the right fit. Finding the group that you feel the most connected to can often take time . . . and that's okay. The right person or the right group will present themselves just when you least expect it, if you continue to put yourself out there.

EVENTS & OUTINGS

If you have multiple children or feel like you aren't ready to commit to a class or any sort of group, then I suggest that you begin researching local events in your area. Whether it's story time at the library or free admission day at the Children's museum, it behooves you to take advantage of these often-last-minute events and activities. You'd be surprised at what you find in your area just by doing a quick Google or Facebook search. Here are some examples of the types of events and activities available: fairs and festivals, arts and crafts, story time, outdoor movie nights or concerts, free museum admissions, puppet shows, play gym hours, and more. And if you really can't be bothered, then just go to a park. No matter where you live, rest assured you will meet other moms there.

I honestly believe that if you're getting dressed and leaving the house, then bravo! That's a big win in my book. Whether you realize it or not, you're putting yourself out there. Like classes and groups, just by being out and about, you've increased your chances of meeting a great new mom friend. Even though you'll probably have more luck at meeting other moms at kid-driven events, you might be surprised where else you might meet them. I met one of my very best mom friends at a Target, bonding over the fact that both of our toddlers were having tantrums simultaneously.

There's no need for you to be alone and struggle through all of motherhood's obstacles solo. You need mom friends for your sanity, your health, and for the enrichment of your soul. Moms need mom friends. Period. Once you find your tribe, it's easier to find self-love because your friends will remind you of just how amazing you are. Women truly have an unbelievable ability to lift each other up, so muster up the strength to put yourself out there and embrace the possibility of creating a new and lasting group of friends. It's empowering to find your tribe, so go get 'em, Mama.

Journal Reflection

Do you feel like you've got a solid tribe? Would you like to make more mom friends? What types of mom friends would you like to meet and where do you think you might find them?

Exercise
SAY GOODBYE TO YOUR COMFORT ZONE

Materials: None
Time Commitment: 45 minutes
Cost: Free

The only way to make new mom friends and find your tribe is to really put yourself out there. Whether you decide to join a group, sign up for a class, attend a local event, or head to the park, it's time to get proactive. For this exercise, I'm going to ask you to approach at least one new mom this week, ask for her phone number, and then follow up. I'm sure you thought you were done dating (if you are attached), but surprise, surprise, you're back in the (mom) dating game again!

FOLLOW-UP QUESTIONS

What was the hardest part about approaching another new mom? Do you think it's worthwhile to continue this practice until you find someone you click with? What sort of potential value do you see in building relationships with other new moms?

Tice Advice:
FIND YOUR TRIBE, FIND YOUR VIBE. WITH THE SUPPORT OF OTHER MOM FRIENDS, YOU MAY BE PLEASANTLY SURPRISED TO DISCOVER WHAT YOU'RE CAPABLE OF AND JUST WHAT YOU MIGHT NEED TO DO TO BECOME A BETTER PARENT, PARTNER, AND PERSON.

"Walking with a friend in the dark is better than walking alone in the light."

Helen Keller

Chapter 5
JUST BE YOU, MAMA

How to Stop Comparing and Start Praising Yourself

"A flower does not think of competing to
the flower next to it. It just blooms."

Zen Shin

Picture this: A former beauty queen with undergraduate and law degrees from an Ivy League institution, married to a charming and kind man of similar pedigree. They pop out five gorgeous children who seem to be nothing short of little geniuses and angels. This mom Superwoman exists. I know her in real life. She's beautiful, inside and out. She commands a room, dedicates her spare time to philanthropic endeavors, and is quite the home baker.

But can you honestly tell me that you weren't a little bit envious of the woman I described above? I know I used to be until I realized that we will never be the same person, never have the same children, and never lead similar lifestyles. I won't achieve what she has, and she won't achieve what I have, but we're both winners in our respective lives.

. . .

Comparison is entirely natural. It's how we innately learn what we'd like to strive for and who we'd like to be. Comparison can provide a framework for understanding if we're on the right track or if we need to make adjustments to achieve certain goals. Comparison can be a catalyst for positive change, career advancement, or even improved health. Unfortunately, comparison can also cultivate feelings of inadequacy, jealousy, insecurity, and more.

Fact is, comparison has the capacity to both inspire and consume, especially as a new mother. Think about it. When you talk to your other mom friends with children of similar age, are you secretly concerned when their child is reading and yours is not (consume)? But then, do you ask them for guidance on how they think you may help your child reach the same level of reading proficiency (inspire)? Are you jealous when their child is wearing Ralph Lauren and yours is wearing Carter's (consume)? But then, once you ask where they bought their child's adorable outfit, you come to find out there's a sale going on at Nordstrom's, and those brands are suddenly within your budget (inspire). How about when their baby sleeps a solid ten hours at night and you're still up every three to four hours consoling yours (consume)? But then, they recommend a book or device that helps your baby sleep better (inspire). It's extremely hard not to compare yourself and your children to everyone else; however, it's imperative that you focus your energy on the inspirational aspects of comparison. Otherwise, you *will* emotionally deplete your sense of self-worth and self-confidence as an individual and as a parent.

On top of that, you should also be extremely careful with how you use and utilize social media. The negative, destructive kind of comparison loop has been magnified by the globalization and infiltration of TikTok, Instagram, and Facebook into our everyday lives. From the moment anyone opens these apps, they're bombarded with pictures, captions, and articles meant to project a grander lifestyle than that which usually ever exists. Most often people post glamorized versions of themselves or their experiences in order to gain a stronger following or an increased number of likes.

Are you guilty of this? I hate to admit it, but I know I am. I get sucked into the negative comparison loop, just like so many others, on social media. I don't go around posting pictures of George post-poopy diaper blow out or of him having a tantrum on the floor of Target (although maybe that would get me more likes?). I post pictures of him smiling or laughing in front of some beautifully manicured landscape or backdrop with gorgeous lighting or flattering filters (yes, that photo easily took sixty captures to accomplish). That isn't a very accurate representation of my daily life. Why do I keep repeating this ridiculous trend and treating my son like a circus monkey instead of a tiny human? Because we all share in our basic need and desire for approval, encouragement, support, and love, but social media isn't the best place to go looking for it.

I wish I were immune to the power that comparison can play in the world of motherhood, but I'm definitely not. I can't help but feel pangs of jealousy on occasion when one of my mom friends is pushing their child in the stroller I'd been longing for or is on the European vacation I wish I had the finances to afford. These platforms can play dirty mind tricks on all of us and lead us down a rabbit hole of dejection if we allow it. Because these apps are overwhelmingly addictive, it makes it hard to break free from the evil that can be born or exacerbated by daily (or even hourly) comparison.

I also need to remind you that things are *rarely* as they seem, and your personal journey is far more important than any of the superficial crap that you consciously or subconsciously digest when you allow these platforms to have control over your feelings. Just keep in mind that time when you were shocked that so-and-so was getting a divorce after posting a wedding picture with a sappy caption a few days prior . . . or that so-and-so posted a picture of their child happily running along the beach but forgot to add the part where they all got COVID on the way back from their trip. So quickly and easily do we scroll and gloss over images and absorb all the wrong messages.

This doesn't just happen on apps and online; comparison is conditioned and unavoidable in everyday life too. But jealousy and judgement will never serve you. It will only destroy any hope you have of leading a more carefree life. At some point you must draw the line, recognize the damage associated with negative comparative thinking, and karate chop it into submission.

HOW DID WE GET HERE?

If the goal is to lead a more fulfilling life, then it's important to address the root from which these ideologies formed. It's not your fault, I promise. It's quite shocking how conditioned we are into idolizing fairy tales, without often stepping back and realizing that they are called "fairy tales" for a reason. Life is messy and complicated, which also makes it beautiful and surprising. There's no question that once you enter motherhood, an entirely new set of comparison categories and feelings will emerge.

I don't know when exactly these unrealistic fantasies began edging their way into your psyche, but that "happily ever after" ending to every Disney movie and storybook pre-1990 is a real doozy. Back in the early '80s (when I was born), from toddlerhood into my teens, women were made to believe that their beauty was their best asset and that living "happily ever after" equated to marrying someone successful, charming, and attractive as well as miraculously popping out a few gorgeous, healthy, well-behaved children. Let's not also forget what these princesses and female characters looked like: huge boobs, tiny waists, ample hips—just like the toys we were also given—namely, Barbie. What a pile of BS, don't you think? How did we fall into this trap of searching for something that doesn't exist as well as having a body that is completely unattainable? How did we allow projected social norms to destroy our sense of self-worth?

Sadly, it's quite simple, really. From Snow White to Teen Vogue, from Victoria's Secret to SlimFast, we are constantly being told that we are not enough. Advertising, publications, retail brands, food companies, and so on are all telling us that we *need* to change. We need to be more beautiful, skinnier, trendier, fashionable . . . and heaven forbid we choose to "age gracefully." They sell us on the concept that if we make said change then we will be happier (a.k.a., live happily ever after).

Have you ever thought to yourself, "If I just lose ten pounds, I'll be so much happier?" I know I have. And you know what? After losing those ten pounds by starving myself and being a witch to everyone because I was *hangry*,[24] I'm not happier or a better wife or a better mother or a better person. Without often realizing it, we have allowed so many marketing and advertising campaigns to subconsciously rewire our brains into believing we want something we either don't need or to be someone we clearly are not.

It pains me when I get messages from moms, like Laurie from Ohio, who are suffering due to these unrealistic expectations: "I think I always feel pressure. I think it's just about my own sense of what womanhood/motherhood is supposed to look like: I'm supposed to be lean and strong, stylish in a pared-down way, making it all look easy. I expect to look like the magazine images of women I grew up with. I

---

24. Dictionary.com, s.v. "Hangry, *(adjective) Slang* – 'feeling irritable or irrationally angry as a result of being hungry,'" accessed August 10, 2021, https://www.dictionary.com/browse/hangry.

find that so many things about motherhood make me feel uncomfortable or imperfect." This, unfortunately, is genius-level marketing at work.

Having spent over twelve years in the fashion industry as a plus-size model, I can tell you how this brainwashing happens seamlessly. I have spent a decade selling the "right" clothes, underwear, jewelry, swimsuits, and what not to the "right" body size, shape, ethnicity, age, and I completely bought into it too until I really understood all of the lies we're continuously sold. Don't get me wrong—I do love the feeling of being pampered and someone taking beautiful pictures of me, but there have been multiple instances where I have projected an image or promoted a product that I deeply regret.

A few specific behind-the-scenes industry standards and anecdotes may help you to come to the same realizations about marketing and sales that I have. Let's start with padding. Padding is exactly what it sounds like. It's a body suit made of pads to give you a specific shape or make you a specific size. You can add or subtract pads to create the "perfect" figure. When you're a plus-size model, most retailers aim to achieve an hourglass figure, so they may ask that I put cutlets (silicone inserts) in my bra or add pads to my hips. I'm naturally a size 12, but with my padding, I can easily make myself a size 14–16.

When sample size clothing doesn't fit correctly, I grab my padding and adjust my shape to fill it out in all the right places OR a professional fashion stylist assists me by pinning the clothes until they appear to be a perfect fit. That usually takes care of about 80 percent of the "imperfections." Then, someone digitally alters the final image, handling that last 20 percent. After that, the image is posted online, on a billboard, in a catalog, or in a magazine to be consumed by you. These bodies, faces, and digitally altered images are nothing but illusions. Can I get a WTF, please? When did it become so normal to project unrealistic body images to the point of absolute flawlessness? When did companies decide it was okay to let women believe that they were buying something that is completely fabricated? Sure, the actual garments exist . . . but it sure won't look like that when you try it on.

Not only that, but certain body "imperfections" have now been negatively labeled and publicized to the point of ridiculousness. Who spends a lot of time looking at themselves from the back? I know I don't; yet somehow, I'm constantly targeted with ads for smoothing back fat. *Excuse me. Back fat?* So now I don't only need to be ashamed of how I look from the front, I also need a special bra or shirt to get rid of every wrinkle or roll I have in the back? I've modeled for these brands before, and it's ridiculous. The clients make me slouch or contort my body in unflattering ways to fabricate rolls I typically don't have. Then, they put on their "special garment" and position me completely upright, while also pinning the front to ensure I have a completely smooth back . . . and I don't know about you, but I couldn't care less how I look from the back, and I think it's cruel that so many brands prey on women who aren't a size zero by making them feel badly about every aspect of their bodies.

From shapewear to wrinkle cream, when are we going to wake up and realize we've been fed lie after lie about what we should look like, how we should live our lives, and what we need to "fix" in order to be happy? It is lunacy and it is *not* your fault that you pick apart your "flaws." You have been conditioned to believe that you have them. I'm here to tell you that you don't and help guide you to the realization that *you rock, just the way you are.*

HOW DO WE SET OURSELVES FREE?

We hear and absorb countless messages throughout our day, but the key to setting yourself free is reframing and acknowledging all the messages you are exposed to. Let's take a walk through what I believe to be the number one most damaging message we assimilate about ourselves projected through offline comparison, social media, print, publication, TV, and film: **I'm not good enough.**

Women are all too susceptible to this message because it's in a brand's best interest for you to believe that you will achieve whatever it is you desire by purchasing their product or achieving a certain lifestyle. If you somehow were to realize that you're in fact much better than good enough, they wouldn't have anything to sell, would they? Unraveling and recalibrating this degrading message is no cakewalk because we're bombarded with it almost every hour of the day. However, if you're able to pinpoint and clarify why you feel this way, it makes it far easier to overcome and conquer. The only person who believes you're not good enough is you, and you have the ability to change that. Jennifer from Texas has the right mindset: "I was shocked when my body didn't 'bounce back' postpartum. I thought it would, but it didn't. I focused my thoughts on how my body allowed me to carry a child, then feed a child, and finally now take care of a child. My body is bigger, but so is my heart."

If you're struggling with body and insecurity issues, it's time to face them head on. Let's go on a little adventure to uncover your inner Queen, Mama!

Journal Reflection

Take a moment and really simmer on why you may believe you're not good enough. (If you believe you are, then bravo! Go ahead and skip to the next chapter!) Does it have to do the comparisons you've been making lately? With your appearance? The way you parent? Your spouse? Your career (or lack thereof)? Why do you truly believe you're not good enough? Do your best to find these answers for yourself, and then jot them down in your journal.

Once you've written them all down, go ahead and make a list of all the things that you're proud of. What are the things you brag about? What aspects of yourself make you feel that special glow? What things have you shared on a first date or a first interview that you believe are flattering qualities you possess?

After you have completed this writing task, go ahead and reread your notes. Do you still believe you're not good enough? I sincerely hope not! But for reinforcement's sake, complete this exercise (compliments of Disney's *Frozen*): "Let it go, let it go, turn away and slam the door!"

Exercise
YOU ARE A WARRIOR

Materials: Journal, pen, pack of 10 balloons, small pad of post-it notes, and thin-tipped (permanent) marker (optional: safety pin)

Time Commitment: 20 minutes

Cost: $10

Step 1: Using the lists that you generated above, jot down and summarize ten negative words that embody what you believe to be your weaknesses. The first ten adjectives that came to my mind were lazy, insecure, overweight, difficult, incompetent, dependent, anxious, worrier, awkward, and boring. Once you determine what your ten words are, go ahead and inflate all ten balloons. Next, write each one of these words on its own balloon (**Tip:** it's easier to write on the balloons after you inflate them, not beforehand.) Then, take 5–10 minutes and watch them float around in your space (just like how they float around in your head). Why are you allowing these negative thoughts to permeate your daily life? How can you abolish these feelings and insecurities? Once you feel confident in your answers to these questions, pop them one by one (with or without a safety pin).

Step 2: To reinforce letting go of the labels that aren't serving you, it's time to acknowledge which labels could be. Writing down your strengths is also empowering. So, take out your small pad of post-it notes and use the first ten sheets to write down ten positive labels that embody what you believe to be your innate or learned talents. Here are some examples: resilient, nurturing, powerful, kind, generous, thoughtful, persistent, determined, tough, energetic, savvy.

Then, when you're done, place them in different spots that might be helpful to you. Maybe you put "Resilient" in your wallet to reference it when your child is having a meltdown at the grocery store, or you put "Persistent" on your desk to remind yourself that you won't let a coveted client take no for an answer. I also suggest putting words like "Powerful" and "Tough" on the corner of your bathroom mirror or in your jewelry box so that you see them more regularly.

FOLLOW-UP QUESTIONS

How did it feel to pop each balloon? Did it make you feel relieved to let them go?

How do you think it might feel if you actively stopped carrying around these negative thoughts about yourself? How can you use everyday comparison to your advantage and allow it to inspire you? Where did you decide to put your post-it notes? Have they helped you to recognize why you're a rockstar?

Tice Advice:
ONCE YOU PUT LABELS ON ANY BAGGAGE YOU'RE CARRYING AROUND AND UNPACK YOUR NEGATIVE THOUGHT PATTERNS, IT'S EASIER TO KICK THEM TO THE CURB.

"For what it's worth: it's never too late to be whoever you want to be. I hope you live a life you're proud of, and if you find you're not, I hope you have the strength to start over again."

F. Scott Fitzgerald

Chapter 6

NEVER UNDERESTIMATE THE POWER OF NATURE

WHY YOU SHOULD MAKE TIME TO HUG A TREE

"Smell the sea, and feel the sky,
let your soul and spirit fly."

Van Morrison

It was 2:00 a.m. on a Tuesday, and my husband was out of town on business. I was alone with George (who was six weeks old at the time), and he would *not* stop crying. I had just fed him and changed him. I had bounced him, rocked him, put his head on my chest, and sung to him. Nothing worked. The crying persisted to the point that I started crying as well. I didn't know what else to do.

I knew my neighborhood was relatively safe, and I felt like I was losing my mind, so can you take a wild guess at what I did? I bundled George up (it was mid-February), grabbed my heaviest coat and boots, strapped him to my chest, and went for a walk (even though it was pitch black outside).

As soon as the cool fresh air hit his precious little cheeks, silence. The crying ceased, and his eyes gently closed. Within two minutes, he was out cold. I couldn't help but let out a huge sigh of relief. It turned out that what we both desperately needed was to get out of the house, regardless of the temperature and the time of day.

No longer was I plagued by the wooshing sound of the breast pump, the whistling of the thermostat blowing heat through the vents, or the stagnant air lingering throughout our home. The streets and sidewalk were empty, and the intense quiet felt euphoric. I could hear the frost on the grass crunching beneath my feet and feel the soft breeze delicately caressing my neck. I could see George's tiny breaths as his chest rose and fell contently. The stars shone brightly next to the crescent moon, without a cloud in the sky. I can thank Mother Nature for saving me that early morning and so many other mornings, afternoons, and evenings. Now I live by the mantra, never underestimate the power of nature. Its healing capabilities far exceed what it is ever given credit for.

· · ·

As difficult as it may be to get your butt out of the house, it is an absolute must. Run. Jog. Walk. Swim. Skip, hop, or prance for all I care. Just do whatever you have to do to get yourself outside, with or without your child. There is nothing else I can think of (besides maybe a few illegal or prescription substances) that can change your mood and overall mindset almost instantaneously. Don't worry, I'm not asking you to run a marathon or go for a rigorous hike. I'm asking you to go look at the trees in your neighborhood, take in the clouds or the stars in the sky, and breathe in some truly fresh air. You can thank me later, but just get up from doing whatever you're entrenched in at this moment and make getting outside a daily to-do of yours. It'll do your body good.

Josefin from California echoed my sentiments: "After having both my babies, being outdoors was the only thing that kept me sane. I was not prepared *at all* for how exhausted I would feel from sleep deprivation and breastfeeding 24/7. Even on the most challenging days, I promised myself to spend time outdoors (even if it was just for ten minutes.) I realized quickly how calming it was, both for me and my babies. The sun and the wind helped me breathe and clear my 'mom brain.' For me, spending time outdoors was (and still is) the best mental recharge, and I'm forever grateful for Mother Nature!"

In the article, "Ecopsychology: How Immersion in Nature Benefits Your Health," author Jim Robbins highlights just how impactful spending time outdoors may be. "Studies have shown that time in nature—as long as people feel safe—is the antidote for stress: It can lower blood pressure and stress hormone levels, reduce nervous system arousal, enhance immune system function, increase self-esteem, reduce anxiety, and improve mood."[25] Not only is it good for you, but it's also something that you should promote to your neighbors. "Studies show that the effects of nature may go deeper than providing a sense of well-being, helping to reduce crime and aggression. A 2015 study of 2,000 people in the United Kingdom found that more exposure to nature translated into more community cohesion and substantially lower crime rates."[26] Now that's something that everyone should get behind!

No matter the age of your child, walks and outdoor excursions are necessary for the mental health of your entire family. No matter how busy my schedule may be, I make sure to take at least one walk, bike, scooter ride, or trip to the park at least once a day. Sometimes it's with George and other times I'm alone. I have come to realize that spending time outside (regardless of weather conditions) is important for my heart and soul. So, whether you have to strap your child to your chest, into a stroller, or into snow boots, it's worth it to make it happen.

I realize that sometimes doing the same things over and over again can become a bit monotonous, so here are some ideas to reference when you're feeling unmotivated to leave

25. Jim Robbins, "Ecopsychology: How Immersion in Nature Benefits Your Health," *Yale Environment 360*, January 9, 2020, https://e360.yale.edu/features/ecopsychology-how-immersion-in-nature-benefits-your-health.
26. Robbins, "Ecopsychology."

the house. These are activities you can do with your child, but also by yourself (to bring out *your* inner child).

- Visit a local nursery and take in the flowers
- Go hunting for a variety of (gross) bugs or cool sticks (my son loves this)
- Download the Seek app and identify and learn about the flora and fauna in your neighborhood
- Grab some sidewalk chalk and make a colorful masterpiece or play hopscotch
- Encourage water play with simple bowls, cups, spoons, and kitchen utensils
- Google all the parks nearby and pick a new one to visit (even if it's a bit of a drive)
- Find a nice spot under a big tree to read a book, journal, or reflect on your thoughts
- Find something inspiring to paint in your backyard/neighborhood (and just do it!)
- Find a place to feed ducks, turtles, or fish
- Start a rock or leaf collection to add to regularly
- Find a new garden/botanical garden to explore
- Start bird watching (purchase a bird book to identify local species)
- Play "Count the…" with your child (ex: number of cracks in the sidewalk)
- Bring out the balls, jump ropes, hula hoops, etc. and get your body moving to fun music
- Bring play dough outside and make molds of leaves or textures in your environment

- Have a gourmet picnic in your backyard (I love doing this one by myself!)
- Anya from Texas recommends designing easy scavenger hunts for nature walks
- Challenge yourself to take different walking, running, or biking routes weekly
- Create a fun obstacle course, race, or challenge
- FaceTime or call someone you miss while exercising solo

Journal Reflection

How might you build outdoor time into your daily schedule? Do you think you might benefit more from working out or walking alone? Or would you prefer doing more activities outside with your child? What are some of your favorite outdoor activities that have fallen by the wayside? Do you think it would be helpful to research some new parks/trails to try?

Exercise
HUG A TREE

Materials: Just your outdoor environment
Time Commitment: 5–10 minutes daily
Budget: Free

It might be raining (or snowing, or a gorgeous sunny day), but regardless of the conditions, I'm going to ask you to take at least five minutes and get outside. If you're having an extra hard day, go ahead and do my favorite thing: literally wrap your arms around a tree. Run your fingers along the bark. Notice the texture. Smell the air. Breathe it in and out. Take off your shoes and feel the roots between your toes. It's amazing how grounded you can feel when hugging a tree.

FOLLOW-UP QUESTIONS

Did this activity help you to de-stress? Did you learn something about your neighborhood or daily environment that you hadn't noticed before? Is this something you think you should commit to doing more often?

Tice Advice:
STOP AND SMELL THE . . . TREE.

"One touch of nature
makes the whole world kin."

William Shakespeare

Chapter 7
GOODBYE
AND HELLO

WHAT OUR CHILDREN CAN TEACH
US ABOUT OURSELVES

"I am not the perfect mother,
but I'm exactly the one my child needs."

Unknown

Before I became a mom, I cared a lot about what other people thought of me. I deeply cared about how I portrayed myself in certain situations, what people might think of my lifestyle decisions and career choices, and about the type of person other people thought I was. I worried about inconsequential and silly things like whether my shoes coordinated with my blouse or whether I responded appropriately to a text or email from a friend or colleague. I genuinely cared a whole heck of a lot about my image, my reputation, my social media following, and my persona. Without realizing it, I had become so wrapped up in caring about what other people thought about me that I forgot to *really* care about what *I* thought. I forgot to pay attention to *my* needs, feelings, desires, goals, and such. I forgot to ask myself imperative questions like "What do *I* think about my choices?", "How do *I* feel about my lifestyle?", and "What makes me the person *I* am?"

Then, I became a mom. Like all new moms, I was thrust into a new role and forced to prioritize my child and put myself second. For quite some time, I fixated on this. I secretly obsessed over my old life, with my old friends, and the "good old days." I reminisced about going out and doing whatever I wanted, whenever I wanted. Then, when George was about three years old, I had an epiphany.

I woke up one morning and realized that I would never, *ever* want to be the old me because the new me was far superior. In only a few short years, George had given me the unbelievably generous gift of teaching me who *I* wanted to be and who I already was. It became clear to me that I wanted to be someone that he admired. I already had my answers.

From his perspective, everything I do and say is magic. Rolls on my belly? Perfect to snuggle in. Gray hairs on my head? Totally gorgeous. Purchasing an adult scooter and flying down big hills, laughing hysterically? Pure enchantment. Crying over a hard day? "It's okay, Mommy. I'm here for you. I'll protect you," George says.

It became blatantly obvious to me that the only opinion I care about nowadays is George's and my own. He doesn't care if my outfit doesn't match. He doesn't care if I don't do everything "correctly." He doesn't care if I didn't have time to take a shower (although he will tell me if I'm stinky!). He doesn't care about any of the superficial things that I used to care about. He loves me for who I am, just the way I am, whole-heartedly . . . and I owe it to myself to do the same. The only person who can lift you up or bring you down is *you*.

So, I decided it was time for me to stop . . . "stop the insanity" as Susan Powter says. It was time to give myself a "mental mom makeover" and embrace the absolute power and freedom I unknowingly gained by becoming a parent. I realized that if I got really quiet and listened to what George had to say about me, I could gain VIP access to unlimited information about who I had become now and why. It also helped me to tap into my own strengths, desires, and aspirations. Children are fabulous reflectors, you know . . . and they tell it like it is, even if it can feel harsh at times. Believe it or not, there's a treasure trove of information just waiting to be discovered, lying in bed down the hall (or next to you, if you happen to co-sleep).

· · ·

What does this all mean? What it means is that you already have a lot of the answers that you're seeking. I'm talking about the person you have become *because* of your child. All you have to do is tap into the resources staring you directly in the face, while also accepting one giant fact about life: It will continue to be a journey until the day you take your very last breath. People will change, circumstances will change, and *you* will continue to change. But I believe that you have it within yourself to fill your life with more joy, acceptance, and self-love. I'm talking about building upon and embracing each version of yourself as you grow. You just need to step up to the plate and keep on swinging, while also prioritizing and appreciating yourself. This means actively listening to what your child has to say about you—really doing your best to acknowledge what they tell you they see, hear, and feel.

Jonelle from California said, "My son loves my hair and eyes, while my daughter hilariously loves my belly button! Even when I think I look my worst, my kids always unexpectedly compliment me." Norma from Florida said, "My boys don't notice much about my appearance, but they love my sense of humor. I always make them laugh by being incredibly goofy and silly."

Who cares if your hair hasn't been washed in days? Who cares if you grocery shop in gym clothes (without ever going to the gym)? Who cares if you say the wrong thing at the wrong time? Who cares if you chicken dance in the middle of Walmart to make your toddler roar with laughter? Most likely . . . no one.

Just like a child, it's time to be unapologetically *you* (all the damn time). It's time to take a page from their book and allow them to be our teachers, guiding us to recognize our strengths when we revert back to counterproductive thinking or behaviors. So, let's dig in. Let's find out more about how you can embrace and embody who you are at this very moment in time.

Journal Reflection

Your friends and family are typically the people who know *you* the best. They may all see you from different perspectives and value you for different reasons. But, for whatever reason, most people don't want to ask their closest allies what they believe makes them great, because it can be perceived as self-centered. However, if you are willing to ask, you may find that they all have different keys to the master lock on your internal treasure chest.

So, take 10–20 minutes and write down what *you* believe others see in you. What do you believe your colleagues think about you? Your friends? Your spouse? Your children? What do you think they would say are your strengths and weaknesses? How would they say you treat them? Why do you think they choose to be a part of your life? How important is it to you to impress the people around you? Why?

Then, take a beat, and answer these questions: Do *you* believe the narratives you just laid out above are true? Why or why not? By looking at yourself from the outside in, what have you learned? Have you found some clarity in understanding who you currently are and who you want to be?

Exercise
CHILD REFLECTION

Materials: Just your "listening ears" (as they say in
   Montessori school)
Time Commitment: 10–15 minutes
Budget: Free

Although it may feel awkward at first, this exercise is an opportunity for you to get a sense of how your child perceives and feels about you. Depending on their age, this exercise looks a little bit different, so I'll break it down for you:

Child Aged 0–3: Instead of directly asking your child about their feelings and perceptions of you, use this time to do one of two things: (1) call a friend or family member and ask them why they value you? What makes you an asset to their life? What type of person do they think you are? Or (2) Write down why you believe you are a great parent to your child. What do you believe they love about you? Dislike about you? What kind of role model would you like to be for them?

Child Aged 3+: At this point, most children have proficient verbal skills, so go ahead and ask them (yes, out loud) these types of questions (in addition to any other questions you may want specific answers to): What do you love about me? Do you think I'm a good mommy? Why? Is there something I could do to be a better mommy?

What do you think I do for work? Is there something you think I need to change?

FOLLOW-UP QUESTIONS

What did you discover about yourself by listening to your child's (or friend's) perspective? What, if anything, do you think you may want to change about yourself or about your lifestyle? Is there any room for improvement?

Tice Advice:

SELF-LOVE AND JOY MUST COME FROM WITHIN, BUT SOMETIMES AN UNEXPECTED TEACHER MAY HELP GUIDE YOU. WHEN YOU REALIZE YOU HAVE THE ABILITY TO DICTATE YOUR OWN JOURNEY, YOU GAIN EMOTIONAL FREEDOM. AND THAT FREEDOM, OVER TIME, BECOMES POWER. AND THAT POWER BECOMES ENLIGHTENMENT AND WHOLENESS.

"If you change the way you look at things, the things you look at change."

Wayne Dyer

Chapter 8

WHEN ALL THE BALLS FALL

WHY TRYING TO JUGGLE TOO MUCH CAUSES A CIRCUS

"Stop wearing more than one hat.
You only have one head."

Melissa Heisler

When George was six weeks old, my best friend decided to fly all the way across the country to help me out for a few days. She could tell I was a complete mess and needed a break, whether that meant holding George while I showered or ordering dinner while I pumped or slept.

On the second day of her visit, she insisted that we get out of the house and go out to brunch with George. After a month of trial and error, I had finally gotten into a pumping rhythm and routine. I knew (almost to the minute) how long I could leave the house before George would need to eat, sleep, or poop . . . and he was one of those babes who loved breast milk (so I wasn't going anywhere for more than two hours). Therefore, I got dressed before pumping, assembled everything I thought I might need in the diaper bag (toys, socks, hats, pacifiers, changes of clothes, you know the drill). The only thing I didn't pack was my manual breast pump, but I knew I'd have ample time to get back to the house before he would need or want to eat again.

As soon as we began to walk, I chickened out on brunch and requested we just go for a coffee and a quick to-go bite instead. (Yes, I was *that* anxious new mom!) She obliged, thankfully. We had a lovely walk and chatted with our coffees happily. George was snuggled peacefully in his stroller, observing all the new scenery before he fell asleep for his nap.

After an hour and a half had passed, I told her it was time to head back. George was almost due for his feeding, and I knew he'd wake up from his nap soon. Already dreading having to carry him up the stairs, I fished around in the diaper bag for my keys. Voila! There they were.

I quietly and carefully put the key into the hole, twisted it, and . . . *snap.* The key broke off into the lock, completely obstructing all the surface area around it.

Complete *panic* set in. OMG. I turned to my friend in hysterics, asking her to call a locksmith, my husband, the fire department, anyone who could fix this issue ASAP. I knocked on my neighbor's door (who was thankfully home and who also had young children) and tried to remain calm. I needed that breast pump *now.* George was going to wake up any minute, screaming for milk, and I feared I wouldn't be able to give it to him.

My husband worked close by and immediately drove home to help. My neighbors tried prying out the piece of the key with a coat hanger, a safety pin, a nail, and a paper clip. My best friend called the closest locksmith, who promised to arrive in forty-five minutes or less.

I was frenzied and frazzled. I thought about breaking a window to get in or kicking in the back door. The idea of starving my baby, even for forty-five minutes, was horrifying. Why hadn't I brought that damn hand pump? Why was this happening? I tried to prepare for everything and now . . . *this*.

I don't know how or what exactly my husband did, but after ten minutes of playing "how the heck can I get this door open by using weird and unusual tools," he unlocked the door.

Tears of relief streamed down my face as I pushed George's stroller through the front door. In that exact moment, he woke up. He was just fine. Happy as can be.

It was me that was a complete disaster. It was me that had put an overwhelming amount of pressure on myself. It was me who was hysterical because I felt like a horrible mother for not being prepared for anything and everything. It was me who felt like I had failed, despite the situation being out of my control. It was in that moment that I understood just how much pressure I was going to feel as a mother unless I changed my approach to motherhood, and fast.

. . .

Juggling. It's a skill and a curse. Reality is, at least one ball will eventually drop (usually at the exact moment you're least expecting it). It's one of the hardest, most frustrating parts of being a mom. We want to do *everything*, but physically (and mentally) we cannot. We want to make that soccer game that inevitably starts at the same time as a work dinner planned weeks ago. We want to pick up our child early from school but somehow wind up late because of (ugh) traffic. We want to make all the perfect Pinterest-worthy Halloween treat bags for the school party, but, um . . . life.

We all have the best intentions and often the highest of hopes, but occasionally, we need to be more realistic with our expectations of our children and ourselves. Does this ring a bell to you? If so, the fact that you're worrying about these things probably means that you're already a pretty freaking great mom . . . and trying to find a balance is pretty freaking difficult. And I hate to say it, but most moms are terrible at delegating (me included) because we want everything to be done *our* way (because it's always the best way, right?).

But let's explore and get specific here for a minute. What does being a "great mother" look like to you? Is it a mom who snuggles and cuddles their kids endlessly? Pushes their kids to succeed *and* volunteer? Teaches their children how to be polite, have amazing table manners, and always be nice? Is it a mom who is never late, enrolls their children in every extracurricular known to man, or makes homemade healthy organic meals for the entire family every day? Now pause. Absorb all of that. That is a lot of crazy mom pressure and responsibility, don't you think? Does that sound just a tiny bit absurd to you, considering that you're talking about babies, toddlers, and children? It does to me. The bottom line is, whether we realize it or not, we all have far too many crazy expectations of what it means to be a "great mother" and meeting all these expectations is most certainly unattainable. Moms are human too.

Let me recap that for emphasis: It's next to impossible to raise a child that is a concert pianist, a straight-A student, a future pro-athlete, and the class president every year in addition to being well-adjusted, socially adept, polite, intellectual, brilliant, gorgeous, and vegan to boot. These expectations are absolutely ridiculous, and we all fall victim to putting these sorts of pressures on ourselves as well as our children daily. What *is* important is that *we love the children we have for who they are, not the children we envisioned them to be.*

This obviously doesn't mean that we shouldn't have any expectations for our children or that they should run rampant and do whatever they please whenever they like, but it does mean that it's *important to step back and start choosing which balls to juggle and which balls to drop.* If we don't make the active effort to prioritize, we will undoubtedly feel lousy and face burnout.

Erin from Washington said, "I actually felt like I was killing it as a parent until I had my second. Juggling two under two years old made me feel like a failure every day for a long time. My girls are older now, and I feel like a good mom most of the time, but I don't think any good mom ever

THE NEW MOM CODE

thinks she is great. We are always trying to figure out how we can do better."

It's important to listen to your child and see if their needs are being met and helping them to achieve the goals they desire for themselves. It's not telling them that they have to be a doctor or a lawyer or go to Harvard or Yale. It's about telling them that they're important and they matter, and you love them for who they are and who *they* want to become. The most well-adjusted children I know are the ones whose parents do one thing really well: show their children that they love them fiercely regardless of their choices, behaviors, and dispositions.

Motherhood is a marathon, not a sprint. As much as we'd like to try to control everything as much of the time as possible, it's imperative that we learn to control only what we need to in order to help them thrive (and that includes letting yourself off the hook when they fail).

None of us are perfect (thank goodness), and therefore, being able to revel in the delight of daily activities is what sets a great motherhood journey apart from a miserable one. Instead of worrying about the future, you must realize that what you do now (in this very moment) is all part of your epic marathon. You better not sprint at the beginning or else you'll be bedraggled, exhausted, and burnt out when your children grow up and leave the house.

The magic and the beauty of motherhood are happening right before your eyes, right now. The begging they do to get in bed with you early in the morning. The persistent asking to go for bike or scooter rides. The request that you cut up their food or tie their shoes. The way they see something for the first time and it overwhelms them, like a rainbow or snow. You have been given the incredibly special gift to explore the world through their eyes, which may be from a completely different perspective than that of your own. You have the ability to guide them, teach them, and inspire them. You're basically Yoda.

This also means that you have to *give yourself more credit and prioritize yourself as well*. I'm sure you're doing everything you can to be the "perfect" mom in the ways that you see fit, but you need to know that you're probably already a pretty freaking great mom. It's *okay* that you don't get everything right all the time and that you make mistakes. It's okay to give yourself a break when you feel you need (or want) one. Renee from Illinois thinks it's important that you "celebrate the successes of every day and every accomplishment and learn to forgive yourself. Parenting is never over, and we learn and grow with our children."

At the end of the day, we all just want healthy and happy kids, don't we? And don't most kids in first world countries learn how to walk, talk, read, socialize, and become functioning (and often successful) adults? As difficult as it may seem to be, it's time to give yourself some slack. You're doing a wonderful job! Don't let anyone tell you otherwise!

Journal Reflection

It's not often that we sit down and really simmer on what matters most to us. Take a few minutes and begin writing a list of all the things that matter most to you and why. Once you've got a solid handle on what those things are and why they're important to you, then focus on the goals and dreams you have for your children as well as the dreams they currently have for themselves (which could be as simple as learning how to swim or learning how to play the guitar). Then, plan how to help them best achieve those goals. Make clear which activities you want to prioritize and what you think would be the most optimal use of your time and theirs.

Exercise
LET YOURSELF OFF THE HOOK

Materials: None
Time Commitment: Determined by you
Budget: Free

Giving up control isn't easy and sometimes it's unpleasant (especially if you're someone who's anxious), but it can also be extremely freeing. In this exercise, delegate one of your daily chores to someone else *or* relieve yourself from a commitment that you find either unnecessary or dull. It's important to remind yourself that your child doesn't *have to* have a homemade meal every night and that you don't *always* have to attend X event that you've been dreading for weeks. You *always* have a choice, and you can't do everything all the time. Start letting yourself off the hook more and see how you feel when you do.

FOLLOW-UP QUESTIONS

What was the best part about not doing the chore or relieving yourself from a commitment you had? Did you have a difficult time giving up control? Is there one thing you could change in your daily routine that *you* believe might make you happier? Why haven't you changed that one thing yet?

Tice Advice:
WHEN YOU STOP JUGGLING AND START PRIORITIZING WHAT MATTERS MOST TO YOU, YOU INHERENTLY FEEL BETTER; AND WHEN YOU FEEL BETTER, YOU HAVE A GREATER CAPACITY TO BE YOUR BEST SELF.

"Efficiency is doing things right;
effectiveness is doing the right things."

Peter Drucker

Chapter 9

CARPE DIEM, MAMA

WHY THERE'S NO TIME
LIKE THE PRESENT

"Do anything, but let it produce joy."

Walt Whitman

For as long as I can remember, I have always been a worrier as well as a wound-up type-A stress ball. This equates to me expecting the worst, hoping for the best, and being far too verbal when it comes to anyone doing anything differently than I would. Full transparency: I am a complete and utter control freak and *it is exhausting*, for both me and my husband. Neither of us truly accepted my "condition" until recently.

It wasn't until one weekday evening, after a bedtime battle with George, that I came to the startling discovery that I needed to make some serious alterations to certain perspectives I held about life and parenting. I was sitting on the couch having a heart-to-heart with my husband and feeling tears well up in my eyes. It had been quite contentious between us for a few days (because you know, #momlife), and we were finally trying to get to the root of some of our issues.

A stream of nonsensical verbal vomit began flowing from my mouth. In a moment of vulnerability, I exposed a glimpse of what my daily thoughts actually looked like. "What if X happens?" "What if Y happens?" A list of what if I can, can't, should, shouldn't, and such questions were on full blast. They all started with a "What if?" and ended with a "When X happens, then I'll be able to relax and calm down."

In that moment, I was fishing for support and empathy, a shoulder to cry on . . . but what I got in response was far more surprising and powerful. My husband looked me dead in the face and said, "Honey, what you are describing to me is life. There will always be successes, failures, deaths, health changes, accidents, and financial shifts, but worrying about them won't change the outcome. You will just *continue to suffer for the rest of your life* if you can't accept that there are certain things you will never be able to control." *Dead silence.* Reread that again.

It became apparent to me that evening that I had learned two very toxic habits, starting from the time I was a child. I had told myself that (a) if I worried enough, I could control X, and (b) that if I stressed myself out enough in my quest for control, then somewhere down the line, I'd feel relief and/or joy.

I had allowed myself to believe *so* many false truths that even I couldn't navigate my way through all of the crap or differentiate it from actual truth. I had been telling myself lie after lie, like I'll be calmer when he learns to eat solid foods, to walk, to read; or when he's potty-trained, when he can speak his feelings and desires in full sentences, when he stops co-sleeping, and so on. The lies I allowed myself to believe were completely sucking the joy out of everything for me, day in and day out. I was beyond furious at myself that I had let so much of my entire life be riddled with so much fear.

• • •

It's often easy to forget that life is happening right now, in front of your very eyes. It's so simple to get caught up in daily routines to the point where you feel like you're sleepwalking Monday through Sunday (and don't get me wrong, I know how important schedules and routines are for children and the sanity of adults), *but* it's also equally important to remember that there may not be a tomorrow. That all those things you hoped you would do, you'll never get the chance to do. We spend so much precious time delaying joy that we could have *right now*. We spend so much time fantasizing about the ways in which we'll achieve that joy and what it will look like instead of seizing the moment to actually accomplish something. We spend so much time worrying about what *could* happen that we can't enjoy all of the wonderful things that *do* happen unexpectedly (like the moment your child takes their first steps). We're so consumed with what the future looks like that we forget to appreciate the beauty that the present holds.

What do you think would happen if you stopped worrying so much? What if instead of making an organic well-rounded homemade meal, you built a fort with your toddler and ordered takeout? What if you decided to do the laundry tomorrow and instead went outside with your child to blow bubbles and ride bikes? What if you took a scenic run around your neighborhood instead of turning on the TV? Do you think you'd regret it?

We spend so much time doing things we don't enjoy and spending time with people we don't particularly like because we worry about the shoulds, shouldn'ts, and the what ifs. Can you imagine what your life would look like if you stopped trying to control so much and you started focusing all your energy on the people and activities you loved? Do you think you might feel a bit more joy? Do you think it's worth fighting for that joy? I certainly think it is.

Yes, chores need to be done, activities are required, and life events will inevitably happen whether you like it or not. But you *do* have a choice about how you mentally frame every aspect of your life. What do you think would happen if you began filling your mind space with optimistic and "glass half full" viewpoints? Do you think it's possible that you might feel happier if you gave up some of your old mentalities and adopted new and better ones?

It's not as hard as it sounds. I promise you that you have the capability to experience joy right now, today. You don't need to wait for anything or anyone. You just need to trust yourself and begin laying a new groundwork for how you want to experience your everyday life. The time is now, not tomorrow. Take a big deep breath, collect yourself, and complete the following journal reflection and exercise. I can guarantee that by the time you finish them, you'll feel lighter and brighter.

Journal Reflection

Take a few minutes and write down some of the lies you tell yourself on a daily basis, either pertaining to yourself or to your children.

Here are a few examples:

- I might as well stop trying to eat healthy or work out. There will never be time for it.
- I'm a bad mom because I lose my temper sometimes.
- I'll never make enough money for my child to go to college without taking on debt.
- If my child doesn't learn to read by the time he's four years old, then he'll never get into the pre-school I want him to attend.

If you're still having trouble with determining some of the lies you tell yourself, ask yourself these questions: What do you worry about the most and why? Are you worried about your parenting style or how you discipline your kids? Do you worry about your appearance or your health? Do you worry about the future as well as your child's development? Why do you worry about these things so fiercely?

Next, answer these questions:

Are any of these lies serving you in any capacity? Are any of them making your life better or more fulfilled? Are they helping you to feel joy or accomplishment? My guess is that they are holding you back from becoming your best, most present self.

So, what next? Look at your list of lies again and see if you can reframe them in a positive, more productive light. Here's the reframing for the examples above:

- I'll make time to work out and eat healthy when my schedule allows.
- Even though I lose my temper sometimes, it's only because I care so much, which in turn makes me a loving, caring mom.
- I am so motivated to succeed in my career that my child will never have to worry about student loans.
- My child is learning at their own pace and any school would be lucky to have him.

Do you see the difference? Do you see how if you reframe the lies you tell yourself, it's more likely that you will succeed and experience more daily joy? I hope so. Do yourself a favor too and revisit the positive stories you've framed for yourself whenever you have feelings of doubt. The only person standing in the way of your happiness and joy is you.

Exercise
NOW OR NEVER

Materials: None
Time Commitment: 10 minutes every day for an entire
week (or more, if your schedule allows)
Budget: Free

Since this chapter is focused on the power and the importance of living in the now, I'm going to ask you to spend
at least ten minutes today completely dedicated to "special
time" with your child or yourself. Repeat this for the next
six days too. Let one of your daily chores take a back seat
and focus on feeling present in the moment, doing something you enjoy. It doesn't need to be anything elaborate.
It could be something as simple as sharing a hot chocolate with your child or dancing around your living room
to your favorite song. Maybe it's taking a bubble bath or
reading a home improvement magazine. Whatever it is,
turn off your cell phone and be wholly present. Give yourself permission to be free of the past and of the future
for those ten precious minutes. Taryn from Washington
prioritizes quality time with her two girls and "often knits,
sews, paints, and hikes with them."

FOLLOW-UP QUESTIONS

How has your mood improved or worsened since you
prioritized ten minutes of your day to "special time"?
Do you see a change in your child's behavior? Is it worth

continuing this new habit? How did it feel to build this block of "special time" into your daily routine?

Tice Advice:
YOU MIGHT AS WELL EMBRACE THE PRESENT BECAUSE YOU CAN'T PRESS REWIND OR FAST-FORWARD ON YOUR LIFE. THIS VERY MOMENT WILL ONLY HAPPEN ONCE IN YOUR LIFETIME.

"Self-care is giving the world the best of you, instead of what's left of you."

Katie Reed

Chapter 10

PURGE AND CLEANSE (THEN BEGIN AGAIN)

HOW TO TIDY UP YOUR LIFE FROM THE INSIDE AND OUT

"The first step in crafting the life you want
is to get rid of everything you don't."

Joshua Becker

S ince George was born, my husband and I have moved five times . . . in less than four years. I'll spare you all of the specific details of where we moved and on what exact timeline, but what I can tell you with utmost certainty is that what five moves equates to is a whole lot of packing and unpacking. It's watching your material items (beloved, superfluous, and necessary) get crammed into cardboard Home Depot boxes, wrapped with clear cellophane, or stacked between sheets of paper and bubble wrap.

I'm not sure anyone really enjoys the act of physically moving from one location to another. Moving, for me, is labor intensive, emotionally draining, and often overwhelmingly difficult . . . *but* it does force me to reassess why I own certain things and whether or not I really need them. There's nothing quite like getting shipping quotes for a single cross-country moving van versus *two* crosscountry moving vans. Those quotes alone are sure to make you take a long, hard look at how many of your possessions you're willing to move and how many you're willing to forfeit.

After five moves in four years (or rather nine moves in ten years), I have learned one essential act to my survival and emotional wellbeing: *purging*. Each time I move, I inevitably must part with at least a portion of my belongings. It also means that I must say goodbye to that chapter of my life. That typically entails not only saying goodbye to the physical space I occupied, but also coming to the realization that certain relationships and friendships will end and that that piece of myself will no longer exist. Moving can often be very painful in that sense, but I don't regret any move that I've made throughout my entire life. Each move has helped me to become the person I am today (and I'm proud of the person I've become). Each move has forced me into a cycle of purging, cleansing, growing, and awakening. Each move has helped me to better understand who and what serves my best interests, aspirations, desires, and goals.

Moving is also the ultimate mental unpacking challenge because it quickly makes you realize that you can only have a finite amount of time in any one place . . . and that time is precious. The time you do have needs to be dedicated to maintaining meaningful relationships, letting go of people who don't appreciate you, and removing both the metaphorical and literal baggage you may have been unknowingly carrying around for far too long.

· · ·

As I mentioned before, I absolutely believe purging is imperative to personal growth.

> **Purge** (/perj/), *verb*, "rid (someone or something) of an unwanted quality, condition, or feeling."[27]

What do *I* mean by purging? I mean being proactive and deliberate about cultivating a home environment that provides joy, cultivating friendships that enhance and enrich my life, and making sure to take the necessary time to check in on myself. For me, this purging is always both physical and emotional.

It means that I *consciously know* that I feel more settled and grounded when my home is uncluttered and tidy. It means that I *know* I have spent my time well when I leave a friendly coffee date with a sore jaw from laughing so hard. It means I feel more at ease with my thoughts when I make the time to journal. It means that I don't let the toys and clothes that George has outgrown pile in a corner. It means that I force myself to get rid of things I no longer use, need, or

27. Google Search, s.v. "purge, (verb)," Dictionary, provided by Oxford Languages, accessed August 10, 2021.

wear (or things that no longer serve me). It also means that I take the time to organize both the material items I possess as well as my thoughts. It means a quarter of my car trunk is usually occupied by at least one box or bag full of items to donate.

It means that in order to reach my fullest potential and harness my highest level of productivity, I know that I need to provide myself with a physical space as well as a clear mindset in which to feel relaxed and unfettered. (Yes, I do acknowledge that there are those rare people who actually feel *more* comfortable with a messy space and function more efficiently when they are in high-pressure situations or mental states, but that's not me.)

Christine, a music teacher from Washington, had a great point: "If you have to purge, then you are spending money needlessly. A place for everything and everything in its place. Too much stuff also makes cleaning difficult. My students would come into my house and comment on how relaxed they would feel."

I think everyone should make an active effort to purge as often as they are willing to. The practice of purging and cleansing is awesomely freeing and eye-opening. You might be surprised by how quickly your life changes for the better in ways you didn't think possible or anticipate. You might also realize that the only thing you can actually count on *is* change and that by vigorously making the time to purge, you allow yourself to get rid of certain baggage that may be weighing you down. But keep in mind that purging is symbiotic. You must both physically and emotionally purge in order to have the biggest impact.

Journal Reflection

How do you think you may benefit from purging? Can you get rid of certain things in your home but just haven't made the time to give them away? List them. Are there specific people in your life that are dragging you down and draining your energy? If so, why are you letting them occupy your space and time? Conversely, are there people you know who you believe could enhance your life? Have you reached out to them to get to know them better?

Exercise
DON'T RESIST THE URGE TO PURGE

Materials: None
Time Commitment: 1 hour
Budget: Free

In with the new, out with the old. In this exercise, I am going to ask you to go into your closet, pantry, child's room, and the garage (oh no!) and commit to donating at least ten items from your household. Yes, a minimum of ten.

This is your chance to *really assess which items you possess are actually assets* (boom!) and get rid of at least a few things that are cluttering your physical and mental space.

The best part? You get the opportunity to help someone who may really need those items. Consider donating whatever you are "trashing" to the Salvation Army, Red Cross, or a local shelter.

Want to kick it up a notch? Use the drive to the donation center of your choice to reflect on any relationships you feel may be weighing you down and determine if it might be best for you to cut ties.

> **A fun hack is also to donate to H&M or Nordstrom! Both stores will take all used clothing/sheets to be repurposed/recycled and in exchange give you a discount or coupon for your next purchase in their store.

FOLLOW-UP QUESTIONS

How did it make you feel to donate ten items in your household? Do you feel lighter getting rid of things you don't need? What did you learn about what you value in your household by actively collecting items to give away?

Tice Advice:
PURGE IS THE WORD.
CLEANSE IS THE VERB.
NO DIGGITY.

"To truly cherish the things that are important to you, you must first discard those that have outlived their purpose. To throw away what you no longer need is neither wasteful nor shameful. . . . A dramatic reorganization of the home causes correspondingly dramatic changes in lifestyle and perspective. It is life transforming."

Marie Kondo

Chapter 11

DITCH THE WINE, FEEL OH SO FINE

WHY ALCOHOL IS NOT YOUR FRIEND

"I understood myself only after I destroyed myself.
And only in the process of fixing myself,
did I know who I really was."

Sade Andria Zabala

After my husband was let go from his second job in eighteen months (by no fault of his own), I was in a pretty dark place. My husband is not only talented, smart, and witty, but he is also extremely hardworking and driven. So this was a big bruise to his ego and an unexpected financial surprise for our family, especially considering that he was the sole provider at the time. I wasn't quite sure what to say, and I also wasn't quite sure I was ready or willing to go back to work and leave George.

At the time that it occurred, we didn't particularly like where we lived. We had uprooted our lives and moved cross-country for the specific job my husband had just been let go from. Luckily, we had money saved in our bank accounts as we contemplated, "What the heck are we going to do now?" We knew that we didn't want to stay in the town where we were currently residing, and we also weren't exactly sure where we wanted to go. We both were thankful that George was only eighteen months old and not enrolled in school yet. That would have made things that much more difficult to digest.

In the end, we did something relatively impulsive. We put our house on the market, booked airplane tickets and an Airbnb in Europe (specifically in Hamburg, Germany), and put the majority of our belongings in storage. Why Germany, you ask? Because I had always had good luck booking modeling work there in the past. I felt it was our best chance at making any sort of income in our unexpected and soon-to-be homeless situation (our house went under contract within three weeks).

So, we flew eighteen hours with an eighteen-month-old (yep, *that* was a traumatic experience) and embarked on a wild adventure, full of joy, elation, depression, anxiety, and shock. I didn't have any modeling jobs booked before we left, and we didn't have a home to come back to whenever we decided it was time to book return flights home. We were winging it, together . . . and it was stressful AF. (Did I also mention that I accidentally booked an Airbnb with a bed that was too small for all of us to sleep in? Damn European sizing! My husband was forced to sleep on a couch for almost three months!)

All the excitement and the "WTF did I just do?" culminated in trip after trip to the liquor store (because that's the European way, right?). We woke up each morning eager to explore our new surroundings but equally concerned about what our future living and financial situation was going to look like. We did our best to stay optimistic and hopeful, while simultaneously drowning our sorrows in scotch and wine.

I was, however, very lucky to have such an amazing German modeling agent. She booked me a job for the day after we landed and provided me with a steady stream of income over the course of our three-month stay. She booked me jobs all over Germany, Portugal, and Italy. She was infinitely supportive and highly motivated to help me work, work, work, work, work. Thank goodness.

After two months had passed and my husband was getting homesick for the United States, we decided to move to a completely new city that we knew very little about (we'd only been there once). We didn't have jobs lined up there, but it seemed like it was family friendly and a great fit for the lifestyle we hoped to provide for George. So, the next thing we knew, we were booking yet another Airbnb in said city for only ten days to give us a little time to find a place to rent and settle down.

As much as this all may sound glamorous in some ways, let me repeat, it was stressful AF. We were living out of two suitcases, homeless, and moving to a new city where we knew no one and had zero job prospects. This again equated to *daily* trips to the liquor store.

It wasn't until five months into living in this new city that I finally acknowledged the dark cloud of depression that was looming over my head. I was waking up in cold sweats, fighting insomnia with a toddler who also hated to sleep, and still trying to figure out what our family future looked like . . . and how we were going to make any real money. This was a hard position to be in and one that I wanted nothing more than to forget about with a bottle of Chardonnay . . . every . . . single . . . night.

I knew that I needed to get some sort of help and fast, because there was no way I could be a loving and attentive mom to George if my head was filled with anxious and depressing thoughts all day and night. I went to see a therapist, and then a psychiatrist, before coming to the realization that maybe the most beneficial thing I could do for myself was to stop drinking.

Stop drinking? Full stop. *That's completely bananas*, I thought. There was no way I could survive all this turmoil without drinking alcohol, right? *Wrong. All wrong.* It's amazing how wrong I was.

· · ·

Please don't shudder (I can see you right now). I'm not judging you, and I'm not going to tell you what to do, but I *am* going to do my best to shed some light on why alcohol probably isn't doing you any real favors. Deep breaths. Open mind. Ready, set, go . . .

First, let me ask you a few questions. Have you noticed that most children's birthday parties and baby showers are open bar? Have you seen parents filling up their empty water bottles with booze to drink at their children's baseball or soccer games? Do you feel like hosting a play date at your house means that your liquor cabinet or wine bar needs to be stocked? These are my observations, and I find them to be a bit frightening. Eren from Texas put it best when she said, "It's not cute sneaking wine during your child's game and then driving them home. It's a felony!"

New research is coming out now that illustrates just how much of an alcohol problem we currently have on our hands, especially as it pertains to women. NPR journalist, Aneri Pattani, has recently brought to light the evidence suggesting that we need to reeducate ourselves about alcohol consumption and fast: "For nearly a century, women have been closing the gender gap in alcohol consumption, binge-drinking and alcohol use disorder. What was previously a 3-1 ratio for risky drinking habits in men versus women is closer to 1-to-1 globally, a 2016 analysis of several dozen studies suggested. And the latest U.S. data from 2019 shows that women in their teens and early 20s reported drinking and getting drunk at higher rates than their male peers—in some cases for the first time since researchers began measuring such behavior."[28]

---

28. Aneri Pattani, "Women Now Drink as Much as Men—Not So Much for Pleasure, But to Cope," Your Health, NPR, June 9, 2021, https://www.npr.org /sections/health-shots/2021/06/09/1003980966/women-now-drink-as-much -as-men-and-suffer-health-effects-more-quickly.

She even goes on to say that "research shows women suffer health consequences of alcohol—liver disease, heart disease and cancer—more quickly than men and even with lower levels of consumption. . . . What's more, despite alcohol's temporary calming properties, it can actually increase anxiety and depression, research suggests; some studies show it may lead to depression more quickly in women than in men."[29]

Unfortunately, with the help of inventive marketing, advertising, and billions of dollars in investment, there has been a substantial shift in our societal perception of alcohol, which is fueling the problem. What once was a special occasion drink has now become an acceptable everyday drink. Celebrating? Pop the champagne. Oh, you're off work early? Let's go for happy hour. On vacation? Another Bloody Mary, please. Watching a football game? Crack open that six-pack of Budweiser. Stressed out? Let's open that bottle of Cabernet. Nowadays, there is every excuse under the sun to drink and I find it rare to attend a children's event where alcohol is not served.

Take a beat here for a moment. Do you think it's okay that drinking everywhere, at all hours of the day, is acceptable? How do you think your child is assimilating this message? Do you think it might be possible that our society has collectively and inadvertently become addicted to alcohol?

From the way I see it, the answer is a glaringly obvious yes. At first, I really didn't want to believe it. It was easier to just keep drinking than it was to stop. After all, alcohol is

29. Pattani, "Women Now Drink as Much as Men."

served and sold almost *everywhere* these days, which means escaping its grasp is no easy feat. It has become the go-to gift to give a party host, the "de-stressor" for dealing with life's daily challenges, the "elixir of life," and so much more.

Emily from Canada struggled with getting sober but was pleasantly surprised by the impact she had on her other mom friends, "Mommy wine culture is really toxic, and it made my early sobriety difficult. It made me feel like I was missing out on something. But, since becoming sober, other moms have reached out to me expressing how much they resent mommy wine culture and how they wished they didn't engage in it. A few of my mommy friends have actually gotten sober or have cut back considerably after recognizing the negative impacts it was having on their physical and mental health!"

And guess what? All of it is just poison with sugar in it (to make it taste tolerable). If you didn't already know, alcohol is ethanol and ethanol is what we pump into our cars at a gas station . . . and if alcohol really "isn't *that* bad" for you, then why aren't you letting your children drink it? Why can't pregnant women drink it? Why are more people dying today from alcohol-related deaths than any other substance (including prescription pain meds, cocaine, and heroin)?[30] I hate to tell you this (because I'm sure you love your wine as much as I did), but it's a cancer-causing, life-shortening, depression-inducing addictive drug. Need a bit more of a push to believe me? Think about how you feel after you've

---

30. "Deaths from Excessive Alcohol Use in the U.S.," Centers for Disease Control and Prevention, last reviewed on January 14, 2021, accessed August 18, 2021, https://www.cdc.gov/alcohol/features/excessive-alcohol-deaths.html.

had *too much* to drink. Is it hungover? Ding, ding, ding. Hungover = alcohol *poisoning*.

Somehow and somewhere along the line, modern society has been brainwashed. We have convinced ourselves that we like the taste of alcohol (a.k.a., gas + sugar), that we need it to cope with life (when in fact all it does is numb and damage our cerebellum so that we're impaired), and that we're not going to have any fun unless we're drinking (which is 100 percent false). I also think most of us turn a blind eye to drunk driving, overconsumption, and the health-related risks. All those studies that attempt to show its benefits are now backpedaling on their claims. Even more recently, the World Health Organization finally came out and said, "Alcohol has effects, both short-term and long-term, on almost every single organ of your body. Overall, the evidence suggests that there is no 'safe limit'—in fact, the risk of damage to your health increases with each drink of alcohol consumed."[31]

There is a reason that billions of dollars are spent annually on alcohol advertising. It's because they're selling you addictive poison and doing their best to make it look irresistible . . . and it's working. Here's a great example for you. If you're at a party and you offer your friend a drink, aren't you a bit surprised when they decline? Isn't your first inclination to assume that they either have a problem or that they're pregnant? And don't you wait for them to provide

---

31. "Alcohol and COVID-19: What you need to know," World Health Organization, accessed August 10, 2021, https://www.euro.who.int/__data/assets/pdf_file/0010/437608/Alcohol-and-COVID-19-what-you-need-to-know.pdf.

an excuse as to *why* they're *not* drinking? Think about that for a second. Shouldn't it be the other way around? Why *are* you drinking?

Let's address that question. It's an important one. Why are *you* drinking? Is it because everyone else is? Is it because you're stressed out? Is it because you have come to like the taste? Is it because it has become a habit? Is it because you're addicted? I don't know about you, but once I started asking myself these questions, I was faced with a harsh reality. I was drinking this poison because I thought it would help me to cope with certain aspects of my life that I didn't know how to deal with and because everyone else was doing it. To abstain felt weird and awkward.

But let's get back to you. What sort of positive effect does alcohol have on you? Does it make you a better, happier person? Does it make you an exemplary role model or parent? Does it lift you up or make you feel great? If the answer to any of these questions is yes, then you are the outlier. Alcohol is a depressant that robs you of quality sleep, great skin, bright eyes, and quite frankly, delight.

You deserve better. I want you to be and feel like your best self. Alcohol is not your friend; it's your enemy. I want you to be more present with your children, to be more aware of yourself and your surroundings, to help you find solutions for your problems (instead of burying them in booze), and to break through to the other side. It wasn't until I stopped drinking that I felt like I truly woke up from the comatose existence I was living day in and day out thanks to Sauvignon Blanc.

Jessica from Michigan decided she wanted more for herself: "The best part of being sober is that I'm able to make better decisions. Just because you messed up, doesn't mean you can't start over and do the right thing. Now my children say I do more things with them, and they like me better without alcohol. I'm hoping they have no desire to drink when they are older. I just did what my parents did when I was growing up. I'm hoping my kids will follow my sober lifestyle now!"

You may not be ready or willing to make the change (which I do understand), but my conscience couldn't leave out this chapter, because becoming alcohol-free changed my life so profoundly from the inside out. The joy, self-love, and freedom I now experience is unparalleled, and I want that for you too. I've been alcohol-free for over two years now and can happily report that we chose to put down roots in Texas after our European adventures. My husband found a great commercial real estate firm to work with, and I have been able to continue to model while chasing my passion for writing.

If you think you can't stop without help, then please seek treatment. Confide in your friends and loved ones. Email me personally. It's time for you to take control. Remember, "The journey of a thousand miles begins with a single step."[32]

---

32. Quote from philosopher Lao Tzu.

Journal Reflection

What do you believe you're gaining by drinking? How do you think it makes you look, feel, or act? How is it serving you? How do you typically feel the day after drinking? Would you consider giving it up? Why or why not?

Exercise
HABIT CHANGE

Materials: None
Time Commitment: 5 minutes
Budget: $15 and under

Habit change is essential to leading a healthier lifestyle as well as becoming alcohol-free (which I hope is a journey you choose to embark upon). That being said, I have always turned to food or alcohol to cope with stress. Obviously, that's not a very healthy choice. In this exercise, I urge you to replace one bad automatic behavior with a positive one. Try this for one week and if it makes you feel good, try to keep it up for a month, a year, or even longer. If you're willing and committed to becoming alcohol-free, here's an example of something to try:

I used to spend $12–15 twice a week on a bottle of wine. Then I thought to myself, what if there was another way to spend that money that might still feel like an indulgent treat? What if instead of buying that bottle of wine, I bought myself flowers?

Now think about that. Can you imagine what *your* apartment or house might look like if you bought yourself fresh flowers instead of alcohol? What about if you kept up with that habit every time you had a craving to buy booze? Just imagine how beautiful your home would look and feel!

FOLLOW-UP QUESTIONS

How did it feel to consciously change one aspect of your automatic routine? Do you think you can maintain this new positive behavior? Are you willing to try?

Tice Advice:
HABITS ARE INCREDIBLY HARD TO BREAK, BUT ONCE YOU BREAK OUT OF A REPETITIVE LOOP, YOU MIGHT BE SURPRISED BY HOW MUCH EASIER IT IS TO MAKE HEALTHIER CHOICES.

"Breaking old habits and forming new ones always takes time, but it is worth it in the end."

Joyce Meyers

Chapter 12
CURING EMOTIONAL HANGOVERS

How to Cope with Burnout

"Burnout is what happens when you try
to avoid being human for too long."

Michael Gungor

Water is pounding on my back, my shoulders, and the top of my head, creating a rhythm of sound against the tile floor. My tears are camouflaged in the steady stream of water leaving the showerhead. I sit cross-legged, naked on the floor, with my head in my hands. I feel completely exhausted, defeated, and drained. All I want is to freeze time and sit here forever, but little fists heavily knock on the bathroom door, and George yells, "Mommy! Mommy! Get out of the shower! I want to play!" My husband presses his head against the bathroom door to tell me he urgently needs to answer a work call, and I need to come out immediately . . . but I really, really don't want to. I feel like I can barely move. I don't want my son to see me this way. I feel like I can't breathe. I'm at my wit's end, but I feel like I must pour all my feelings down the drain, just as I turn the showerhead off. I wrap myself up in a towel, take a few big, deep, shallow breaths, and open the door with a smile and a hug for my son.

Fast forward to 3:00 a.m. and my eyes are wide open. My mind is racing, even though it's deafeningly silent in the house. I am in problem-solving mode, scrolling through article after article about how to fix, change, or improve George's recent erratic behavior. He's been out of control, and quite honestly so have I. I Google things like, "how to calm an aggressive toddler," "how to stop a toddler from hitting," as well as "how to survive living with a threenager" and "does parenthood get any easier?" Then, miraculously, I'm able to power down and fall asleep . . . only to be awakened thirty minutes later by George tugging at my arm to tell me he needs help going to the potty. My eyes are bloodshot, my head is groggy, and I feel crushed. Will I ever get a good night's sleep? Will I ever be able to solve these issues? I feel like I can't take even one more minute of sleep deprivation, frustration, and overwhelm. I feel like I'm drowning and all I want to do is lock myself in the closet and cry.

I know in my heart that there's no one I love more, but I also know deep beneath the mom label, I'm also me. Amanda. Amanda who had a whole different set of priorities and goals only a few short years ago. I'm also a person with emotional needs and someone who has always needed and thrived on having alone time. When is it going to be

Amanda's turn for a time out? When is Amanda going to feel like she still exists?

. . .

This, mamas, is called burnout.

Burnout (*noun*): "physical or mental collapse caused by overwork or stress."[33]

Burnout is very real . . . and sometimes even very scary. Burnout can lead to poor decision-making, impulsive behavior, and extreme physical distress. Burnout is typically inevitable for parents because parenting is, in fact, a full-time job filled with stressful decisions that must be attended to daily. As Paula from Arizona put it, "I think being a parent is so hard because we are asked to put the kids needs before ours every single day, day after day (and sometimes our spouses too!). It is mentally, physically, and emotionally exhausting. We wear all the hats—cook, maid, emotional support, chauffeur, referee, laundress, diaper changer, nurse-maid . . . it's like working 24/7 doing a ton of different jobs all at once. When you get to 'clock out' of a regular job, you get to hopefully disconnect and recharge a little, but parenting never has a 'clock out' button. Even when you're not with your children, you're still thinking or worrying about them. Not being able to fully disengage and recharge makes parenting burnout a very real thing."

---

33. Lexico.com, "burnout (noun)," powered by Oxford, accessed August 10, 2021, https://www.lexico.com/en/definition/burnout.

No matter how hard we try or how much we stay on top of current scientific research, it is important to remember a few things about parenthood:

1. LIKE PAULA POINTED OUT, IT'S JUST REALLY, REALLY HARD BEING A PARENT SOMETIMES.

There's no way around it. Some days it may feel like there is actual steam coming out of your head and you swear you have physically been deflated like a balloon. There is sweating, screaming, crying, rage, hugs and kisses, sadness, euphoria, and everything in between. For a toddler, there's also hitting, scratching, biting, yelling, and full-blown meltdowns. It's *hard* when you love someone so much you're willing to give your life for theirs. All you want is the best for them, but they can't possibly understand or appreciate that yet. At some point, you must accept that these types of days are unavoidable, and believe it or not, surviving through them helps to make you a better, stronger, and more resilient parent. It forces you to learn new coping mechanisms and strategies to face not only your fears and anxieties but theirs as well.

These days also force key introspection into your relationship with your family. Think about that for a minute. If these types of days are happening a lot more frequently than you'd like, do you think it may be because you may be trying to control too much? Are you giving your child enough space to be as independent as they desire to be? Are you giving yourself enough "you time" so that you can physiologically remain calm when tantrums begin?

It's absolutely true that you can't avoid these outbursts and big emotions completely, but part of remedying burnout is helping yourself to make parenthood just a little bit easier so that these catastrophic days don't consume you. It takes time and work to get to the root of the issues that make parenting so difficult, but don't stop pushing to find the right solutions for you and your family. It'll be worth it in the end.

2. WHETHER YOU LIKE IT OR NOT, YOU ARE THEIR MOST INFLUENTIAL TEACHER.

I know this adds fuel to the fire when it comes to the pressure you may already feel as a parent, but it's something to just keep in mind. From watching you, your child is actively learning about what the true landscape of the world really looks like. Some of the most highly functioning adults don't know how to deal with big emotions, so why do we expect as much from children? Just like certain feelings and events can be incredibly hard for us, it's incredibly hard for them too. They don't understand why they can't have their way, or behave certain ways, or have certain things. People can be cruel, unjust, and mean. Rules can feel suffocating, ridiculous, and unnecessary. The world can make you feel unloved, lonely, and unimportant.

As much as most of us would like to ignore these facts, they are in fact, facts. The only thing we have control over is how we personally handle these feelings and situations and how we parent our children to do so. We can't promise them that they will never get hurt, nor can we promise them that they will succeed (as much as we desperately want them to).

But we can be positive role models for them and help them to overcome their challenges. A child often reacts to a situation or an environment in the same way that their parents do. Taking the time to teach them, encourage them, and support them as they navigate the hard truths of the world isn't easy, but it's worth investing the time now instead of paying for it later.

Let's also not forget that we are shaping and forming tiny humans who have the capability to become Nobel Peace prizewinners or, conversely, thieves and criminals. It is our duty as parents to try our best, even when we don't want to . . . and to love ourselves enough not to let our challenges define us, but instead our triumphs through pain and adversity. We can't control who our children will become, but we can control how we behave toward them and what kind of examples we set.

3. REMEMBER: SELF-CARE IS NOT SELFISH.

How do we cure our emotional hangovers? By recognizing that we have certain fundamental needs that must be met. I feel like moms almost always feel guilty for having "me time," yet they underestimate just how essential it is for their own health. There's a reason why every airplane safety video on the planet instructs you to put on your own oxygen mask before assisting others. It's because you're no good to anyone if *you* can't breathe. The same thing applies to motherhood. If you don't make that essential time for yourself, you'll always be projecting frantic, negative, stressed-out energy onto your family as well as sucking the joy out of the time you *do* spend with your child. If you really let it get out of control, then you might even begin resenting your child (when it is not their fault!).

If you're experiencing true burnout, then it's time for you to carve out some "you time." Sure, the timing may be inconvenient. Or it may be uncomfortable asking a friend for help or spending money earmarked for something else. But I can guarantee you that if you don't make time for "you time," it's more than likely that your quality of life and mental health will only continue to suffer.

In truth, by taking really, really good care of ourselves and recognizing burnout, we open the door to becoming more compassionate and patient teachers and cheerleaders for our kids. Let's take the necessary time we need for ourselves so that we can raise our kids to be kind human beings. Let's prioritize both us and them above all else.

I also want to point out that *it's okay to not be okay.* If you recognize that this is the case for you and you constantly feel like you're drowning and burnt out, it's time to seek out professional help. Schedule an appointment with a therapist or psychiatrist. Acknowledge that there are ongoing issues you need to address . . . and the sooner the better. Talk therapy works. Medication works. Support groups work. Try one, and if it doesn't work, try another, and keep trying until you find something that works for you. Trust me, *you deserve to feel great!* There are a variety of options out there to help you get to this point.

Journal Reflection

Are you experiencing burnout right now? What does it feel and look like? Are you willing to make the necessary changes to alleviate the enormous amount of pressure you're putting on yourself?

Exercise
YOU DESERVE SOME "YOU TIME"

Materials: None
Time Commitment: Determined by you
Budget: Free (or paid babysitter)

If you are currently in active burnout or you're having burnout symptoms (like "brain fog, limited tolerance [shorter temper], increased stress levels, depression, feelings of isolation, poor sleep, or obsessive-compulsive tendencies"[34]), it's time to prioritize yourself. You may feel guilty or selfish for needing this time, but, Mama, you deserve this time. In this exercise, I want you to pick one of your favorite types of "you time" and make good on your promise to follow through despite possible scheduling changes and/or financial concerns. Read a magazine in the bathtub for an hour. Go see a movie by yourself or with a friend. Get a massage. Take a drive to a quiet place that makes you feel at peace. Go rock climbing. Whatever it is that you need

---

34. "What to know about parental burnout," Grow by WebMD, accessed August 10, 2021, https://www.webmd.com/parenting/what-to-know-about-parental-burnout#1.

right now to feel like yourself and give yourself a much-needed break, do it. Drown out any haters and *enjoy* this essential time.

FOLLOW-UP QUESTIONS

What activity did you choose to do and how do you feel now? Do you still feel burnt out after having some "you time"? If you do, do you think it's worthwhile to carve out additional time to help you cure your symptoms? Do you think it may be helpful to seek out professional guidance? Would you consider incorporating more "you time" into your daily, weekly, or monthly routines? Do you think more "you time" could substantially improve your overall health?

Tice Advice:
BURNOUT IS REAL.
DON'T IGNORE IT. FACE IT HEAD ON.

"It's not selfish to love yourself,
take care of yourself, and to make
happiness a priority. It's necessary."

Mandy Hale

Chapter 13
THINK YOU'RE ALONE? THINK AGAIN

HIGHLIGHTING COMMON STRUGGLES MOTHERS FACE

"Because there's nothing more comforting that someone who actually gets it. Really gets it. Because they've been to the same hell as you have and can verify you've not made it up."

Holly Bourne

Truth-bomb train coming through! Choo choo! I can honestly say I've done the following things in the four years since George was born: Let him eat food off of the floor (five-second rule, anyone?), let him sit in a diaper a little too long (I really, really didn't feel like going home), watched him eat sand/dirt at the playground (it builds their immunity, right?!), locked him in his room for misbehaving, allowed him to watch six-plus hours of movies/TV in a row on an international flight, and spent more than a few days feeding him copious amounts of junk food because it was a special occasion (or I didn't have time to stop at the grocery store that day). I have bribed him, lied to him, threatened him, and yelled at him (all for very good reasons, of course). And you know what? I'm definitely *not* the only one.

What I am trying to get at here is that we can't be perfect parents (or people, for that matter) all the time. It is absolutely, completely *impossible*. It's time for us moms to all come clean about our shortcomings, collectively and openly. There is far too much judgment and secrecy when it comes to parenting, which unfortunately can lead to depression or even suicidal thoughts.

Vera from Illinois shared, "I did feel a distinct sense of loneliness when I first became a mom. None of my closest friends were moms yet, and I hadn't discovered that making the right kind of mommy friends would be the key to my sanity. The world of motherhood can be a tricky place to navigate if you aren't prepared for handling all of the incoming advice, commentary, imagery, and subtle or not-so-subtle references to what you 'should' be doing."

As mothers, we often feel the need to share our triumphs more than our failures. We're happy to trade advice on sleeping or eating habits, but rarely do we discuss the extreme feelings of loneliness, frustration, and inadequacy that come and go with all the responsibilities we bear. So many mothers feel alone in their parenting journey, needlessly labeling themselves as "bad moms," because they feel they have a name or an image they must protect. Did you know that, according to a recent study, "90 percent of mothers feel lonely since having children and 54 percent felt 'friendless' after giving birth"?[35] Or, that in some parts of the United States, as many as one in five women experience postpartum depression or "baby blues"?[36]

In my experience, I have found that so many mothers have it all wrong. We are not alone in our experiences at all. Most of our experiences, in fact, are very common and hysterically normal. You are not the first mother to experience whatever hardship you may face. My guess is that there are many, many more before you who have walked a similar path; they just haven't told you about it.

Far too many topics are taboo, and far too many societal "norms" aren't in fact norms at all. We have mindlessly been fed a lot of BS through television, publications, and social media that alter our perception of the good, the bad, the ugly, and everything in between. (Think about it: Is it *ever* in the best interest of a marketer for you to be content or happy? Of course not! That would mean you aren't buying what they're selling.) So, I'm going to ask you to put up your fists, wind up, and beat the crap out of these unrealistic ideologies that we explored in earlier chapters.

35. Leah McLaren, "The Excruciating Loneliness of Being a New Mother," *Today's Parent*, March 22, 2018, https://www.todaysparent.com/baby/postpartum -care/the-excruciating-loneliness-of-being-a-new-mother/.
36 "CDC research shows that nationally, about 1 in 8 women experience symptoms of postpartum depression. Estimates of the number of women affected by postpartum depression differ by age and race/ethnicity. Additionally, postpartum depression estimates vary by state, and can be as high as 1 in 5 women," "Depression Among Women," Reproductive Health, Center for Disease Control, accessed August 10, 2021, https://www.cdc.gov/reproductivehealth/depression /index.htm.

You have so much more to share and offer than you may even realize. You have the ability to control your narrative and I'm going to show you how. I want you to wake up with a smile on your face and feel joy in your heart. Yes, some days will be easier than others, and some days you will really screw up . . . but you know what? That's okay. You're not alone in your journey, and you should never have to feel like you are.

I have found over the years that the best way to conquer these feelings of frustration and inner angst is to share them. For me, there is nothing more liberating than sharing the cold, hard truth. There's no need to hide behind smoke and mirrors. This is what "real life" is. Why shouldn't it be openly discussed?

The best thing you can do for yourself is to call up a girlfriend or support person (whoever that may be) and tell them all the crazy details of your day. Share *everything*. No, don't just tell them that you're having a rough day. Tell them *all* the events that occurred and all the things that it made you feel. Don't be afraid to tell them your fears, anxieties, and "dark thoughts" in addition to your small and big victories. Chances are, they are dealing with the same trials and tribulations you are, and they will feel a similar relief when you open yourself up to them. I can attest to the fact that some of my very best friends are the people who know my deepest, darkest secrets because we have formed a unique bond with our unrelenting honesty with one another. Being completely frank and sharing your worries, opinions, and reservations with your family or peers can awaken a deep level of connection to them and may also help you to face your inner fears and your mistaken "inadequacies." I tell my mom just about everything. She's a wonderful listener, cheerleader, and truth teller. I don't know what I'd do without her helpful insight and support! Moms really are the best, and we are all far too hard on ourselves!

My guess is that when you "signed up" to be a mom (otherwise known as getting pregnant), there wasn't a lot of transparency about what your daily life might look like after the baby was born. I don't remember the advertisement for the job mentioning preparing an endless number of meals or cleaning up potty accidents, vomit, broken glass, and spills. And it didn't mention driving from point A to Z a million times a week to get to music, art class, or soccer practice; or doing more laundry and dishes than seems humanly possible; and also being a role model of hope, prosperity, love, and success. Chances are, you may not have realized that you unassumingly took on the positions of child waste management, full-time unpaid family chef, housekeeper, nurse, dental hygienist, accountant, human calendar, and event planner. Juggling all those jobs means that it's absolutely normal for you to want to pull your hair out sometimes (or even lose it due to stress) . . . and that it *should* be the norm to bitch to your friends about the limitless number of daily chores that have to be accomplished to keep your household running. Let me repeat, you are not alone in your struggle.

The trick here is realizing that every day will be different and that, every day, all you can do is *your* best. There's not a global parenting competition going on right now (at least as far as I know). Didn't have time to make a fabulous dinner for your family tonight? Big whoop. You were running late, and your child missed the bus? Big whoop. Sometimes, it's best to accept that it is what it is.

Allowing yourself to share your experiences with your friends openly and honestly, however, is one of the best gifts you could give yourself. There is no greater joy than being able to truly be yourself and being loved for who you are, just the way you are. (And hey, if your "friend" doesn't accept you after you open up, lose 'em. They're the ones missing out!)

Journal Reflection

I think it's important to understand the scope of what motherhood really entails and just how much you take on during the day, week, and year. In this journal reflection, I want you to answer the following questions: What daily chores are you responsible for? How do those chores affect your mood and spirit? Do you feel alone in your journey as a parent? If so, why? Are there things you feel you could change that would help to make your experience as a parent (or wife, or daughter, for that matter) better? Then, check in with yourself. Would openly sharing your thoughts and feelings with a peer or family member help to alleviate some of your stress and anxiety? If so, with whom? Why? What would you want to tell them?

Exercise
SCHEDULE A MOM DATE

Materials: None.

Time Commitment: 1 hour

Budget: $5 (to meet for coffee) or $20 (to meet for lunch)

As much as calling up or texting a girlfriend (or support person) to share your feelings is the quickest and easiest way to connect, there is no substitute for one-on-one time in-person. Although it may be harder to say certain things to someone's face, it is necessary to deepen your bond or connection with them. So much of the things we feel go unsaid or are misconstrued through text messaging. I believe so many of us feel alone far too often because we don't prioritize getting together with our friends and family *in person*. I know it takes active effort when there is usually very little energy to go around. However, how much better do you typically feel *after* spending quality time with a friend and sharing your experiences? My guess is a whole lot better.

In this exercise, I'm asking you to schedule an in-person date with a friend. No excuses. Set a date and time, show up, and share something with them that you may have been keeping a secret. Be whole-heartedly honest about something that has been troubling you and be willing to listen to their advice and personal experience. Unless your house is on fire or your child is home sick, don't put this one off. This is the type of self-care all mothers need.

So, grab your calendar and pick up the phone to put something on the books.

FOLLOW-UP QUESTIONS

After you met up with your friend, how did you feel? Were you able to share everything you wanted to share? Could you have shared more? Is this the person you want to share more with, or is there someone else you feel might better understand you?

Tice Advice:
A PARTY OF ONE IS NO FUN.
WHAT YOU DON'T KNOW AND
DON'T SHARE MAY IN FACT
EMOTIONALLY DROWN YOU.

"When we only share successes, we build walls.
When we also share failures, we build bridges."

Jill Savage

Chapter 14
ALL GREAT THINGS COME TO AN END

Why It's Important to Address Death

> "Death is not the greatest loss in life.
> The greatest loss is what dies
> inside us while we live."
>
> *Norman Cousins*

Prior to getting married and having George, it was routine for me to travel internationally. So when my phone rang soon after I landed in St. Croix, I was a bit startled. I had been booked to shoot an editorial for a well-known magazine and had just begun unpacking my suitcase in the hotel room when my mother's number flashed on my screen. Once, then twice, then three times. I was afraid to answer the phone. As I picked up her call, I took a deep, shallow breath in and out. She promptly informed me that my father had been placed on life support since most of his major organs were beginning to fail. She didn't know how much time he would have left and wanted to know how I would feel if she were to need to take him off the ventilator.

I was paralyzed with fear and panic, stricken by the actual reality that my father might cease to exist. He had been sick with blood cancer for years, yet I had somehow managed to convince myself that he would not only pull through, but that he would also one day return to his old self. He had fought aggressively to live, trying numerous experimental treatments and consistently surviving bleak prognoses.

My mother's call, however, came as a surprise. My father had seemed to be substantially improving over the past week, so much so that he had gone from barely walking with a cane to vigorously washing his beloved 1957 split-window corvette in the backyard. I couldn't wrap my head around the words that were coming out of my phone.

"Hello? Amanda? Are you okay?" my mom repeatedly asked as long stretches of silence would fall in between her questions and my answers. I couldn't process or fathom any of it.

I also simultaneously panicked that I was now a twenty-four-hour-plus flight away from both of them (they lived in Hawaii). My head began spinning out of control. Could I get there in time? Would he wait for me? What would I tell the production team and crew? They had flown me from New York to St. Croix, and the shoot was scheduled to begin the next morning. They hadn't booked any other models and wouldn't be able to get another model to St. Croix in time.

I would cost them thousands of dollars if I had to unexpectedly leave. This was also the biggest editorial I had ever booked, and one that very well could change the trajectory of my career. What would my father want me to do? What would he do? Was this *really* his time to go?

I agonized over the decisions I was being forced to make and cried for hours and hours. I felt desperate and lost. I did my best to analyze every aspect of the situation only to feel differently an hour later.

My mom talked me through everything, and we agreed upon a plan. She would wait to take my father off the ventilator despite how difficult it was for her to see him that way. I would stay in St. Croix and complete the two-day job, because we both knew that was what my father would have wanted.

It was an excruciating, heart-wrenching, soul-crushing, and exhausting two days. I did my absolute best to be as professional as possible with the client and to stay calm while I was on location. It hurt in the pit of my stomach and my eyes burned, waiting to explode in a cascade of tears at each day's end.

Somehow, and with the help of my father's energy, I pushed through it. Quite frankly, I could physically feel him with me. I felt him in the sun, in the ocean, on my face, in the breeze, in everything. I felt his comforting energy envelop me in a full body hug. There was no question in my mind that he was there with me even though his body lay motionless in a hospital halfway across the world. I also instinctively knew that he would wait for me. I knew he wouldn't leave without saying goodbye.

After the job was complete, I began my intense trek home. After a full day of flying, I went directly to the hospital from the airport. There he was. My beloved daddy. The man who taught me more than I could ever express in words but who wouldn't have the opportunity to walk me down the aisle. The man who showed me what courage, strength, and perseverance looked like. The man who adored me from the moment I was born and whom I adored equally.

After three long and agonizingly painful days in St. Croix, I sat by his bedside and shared with him some of my favorite memories of our time together as I choked back sobs. I climbed in his bed and held him. I couldn't bear the thought of losing him, but I knew his time had come.

The nurses removed his ventilator and asked that we wait outside until his breathing began to dissipate, and he was more comfortable.

When they came out to inform us that he might only have a few more minutes left, my mother was in the restroom, and I rushed directly to his bedside. I told him over and over again just how much I loved him and then tightly squeezed his hand. In that exact moment, I felt his energy and love transfer to me . . . just as his heart stopped.

• • •

Here's the cold hard truth: we are *all* going to die. Most of us mortals aren't really sure how to cope with that fact, so we find ways to emotionally bury it or avoid talking about it. It doesn't fall under the "fun things to chat about with a girlfriend" category in any sort of social situation. The concept of death is often perceived as dark or ominous as well as forbidden to discuss.

Well, I'm here to tell you that *not* talking about death just might be the very thing that's holding you back from your greatest potential, invention, or success. As mothers, it is impossible for us to ignore the fear of death as it pertains to our children. It may come in the form of, "What will happen to my child if something happens to me?" or "How could I live if something happened to my child?" or "Will my child be safe and well-taken care of in my absence?" These are very real and very frightening thoughts. They are also very common. The problem with them? They are 100 percent joy sucking. It's extremely hard to live a happy and carefree life unless you accept the reality that one day your adventure will end.

Before I came to this conclusion myself, I can't tell you how much time I spent worrying. Worrying I might die and leave my child motherless. Worrying my child might die. Worrying that my husband or my parents might die. I worried day in and day out, allowing a subconscious loop of toxic thoughts to occupy and devour a large portion of my time and energy. My thought loop consisted of questions like: "What if I get into a car accident and die?" "What if a gunman comes to my son's school?" "What if my husband has a heart attack or my mom gets diagnosed with a terminal illness?" "What if . . . what if . . . what if . . .?" And guess what? I hate to tell you this, but they will all die, in some way, at some point, most likely in a situation that I will have no control over. Such was the case for the passing of my father, who sadly never got the opportunity to meet George (who looks so much like him.)

Far more often than not, we don't get to choose when or how we will go either . . . but what if I do this? Or that? Nope. No. It won't change the fact that you, as well as all the people you love, will eventually die.

It's completely okay for this fact to entirely horrify you. It horrified me too at first, but there's very little I can do to prepare for it (besides writing up a detailed will). Trust me, *no one* wants to die prematurely, unexpectedly, painfully, and so on, but chances are, you won't have any control over how you go.

Sooooo, since it's a fact that it *is* going to happen at some point, wouldn't it be far more productive, empowering, and fulfilling to stop worrying about the how and when? To instead take *life* into your own hands and start living more fearlessly? We only get one life. One journey. One fabulous story to tell and to be told by those we leave behind.

Would you rather be remembered as the worry wart or the endless dreamer? The scaredy-cat or the adventurer? The one who played it safe or the one who took new and exciting risks? The hermit or the world traveler? *You* have the power to choose. *You* get to determine how you want to live. *You* can achieve and accomplish whatever it is that your heart so desires. But you must first set your mind free and kick fear and worry to the curb! There's no better time to do so than *now*.

Truth is, we all possess a certain amount of fear when it comes to the unknown, especially in terms of death. The key is to not omit your fear altogether (as that's probably unrealistic for any human being to do), but to instead stop giving it the time of day and disempower it. It is what it is. In a true quest for self-development, you have no choice but to accept what death means. Unfortunately, no amount of worrying or compulsively stressing out will change the eventual outcome. But you may assuage some of your fears by being proactive.

If you regret something that you can now change, figure out how to let it go or fix it. If you're worried that you might no longer be able to financially provide for your family, you can sign up for a comprehensive life insurance plan that would ensure their financial security. If you haven't determined who would become the legal guardian of your child in the event of a tragic accident, you should take the time to identify those people, discuss it with them, and get their approval. If you're distraught at the idea of leaving your child behind, then maybe it's time to write a letter to them expressing just how much you love them or how proud you are of them. Alisa from New Jersey explained that after her son was born, it was time to "save more and put aside money for him. We even considered moving to provide him with a better life." As you can see, there *are* ways to prepare for your death that can alleviate your fear of it, all of which can be accomplished while you're still alive!

Journal Reflection

It's time to hash out your deep-seated fears about death. I know this is an uncomfortable exercise for most, but how can you expect to grow if you aren't willing to explore the reasons *why* you are so fearful? Are you afraid that death will be painful? That you might die with regrets? That you will leave your child or spouse prematurely? That you won't have made an impact on the world? Then, reflect on what you can do to alleviate your fears.

Exercise
WRITE A WILL

Materials: Paper and pen OR phone/computer with word capabilities
Time Commitment: 1 hour +
Budget: $89+ (Trustandwill.com)

I know this is a big ask and a big spend, but I don't think you can put a price on setting your mind free. If you haven't already written a detailed will that describes where you want your assets to go, who you'd like for your child's guardians to be, and what you would like to be done to celebrate or commemorate your life, then this is an absolute *must*. A will provides peace of mind and is also a legal assurance that the people you love will be taken care of in your absence. Don't put this one off. Did you know that "in 2017 almost half (42%) of all Americans said that they have a will or another type of estate planning document?

Fast forward to 2020, and less than one-third (32%) say they have one or more documents—that's a decrease of nearly 25% in just three years. This indicates that while many people know they should have a will, they may also feel like they can put off creating a will until later in life, which can have major consequences in the event of an unexpected death."[37]

(**Major kudos to those of you who have already done it!!**)

FOLLOW-UP QUESTIONS

How did it feel to finally solidify arrangements for your loved ones after you die? Do you feel a sense of relief knowing that you have some control over what happens when you're gone? Are you any less afraid of death now than you were when you began reading this chapter? If not, can you come up with any personal solutions to tackle your fears?

Tice Advice:

FEAR CAN STOP US FROM TRULY LIVING, YET DEATH IS INEVITABLE. WHY NOT **CHOOSE** TO LIVE EVERY DAY TO ITS FULLEST?

---

37. Statistics taken from *Caring.com* in combination with *trustandwill.com*, accessed on August 10, 2021, https://trustandwill.com/learn/trust-will-partners -with-caring-com-on-2020-will-study.

"Our death is not an end if we live on in
our children and the younger generation.
For they are us; our bodies are only
wilted leaves on the tree of life."

Albert Einstein

Chapter 15

FINDING JOY IN THE MUNDANE

HOW TO MAKE
MONOTONY MARVELOUS

"Enjoy the little things in life . . . for one day you'll
look back and realize they were the big things."

Robert Brault

It was a Sunday morning and I had made the mistake of
staying up too late the night beforehand with my husband.
We were having such a blast singing karaoke with my son's
Fisher Price toddler microphone that I just didn't want to go
to bed. As midnight rolled around, my husband passed out,
and I lay awake smiling from ear to ear for another hour
thinking about how incredibly lucky I was.

Then, when my son unexpectedly awoke up at 3:00 a.m.
and called me into his bedroom, I was shattered. I somehow
pulled myself out of bed, went into his room and snuggled
up next to him, falling into a deep sleep with his little arms

and legs wrapped around me. It was a mere two hours later that he was bright eyed, bushy tailed, and wide awake. (I don't know what it is about babies and toddlers, but they should win the award for the world's most extreme early risers.) On an average morning, I'd beg for him to let me go back to sleep, to spend some time playing in his playroom alone, or encourage him to talk to and feed his fish. I'd plead with him to just *please, please, please* let Mommy sleep a little bit longer. Just another thirty minutes. Another ten minutes. Another two minutes.

On this morning, however, an idea popped into my head. I was always shooing him away in my quest for more sleep, and it wasn't *his* fault that I had stayed up so late. It was mine. So in an effort to allow my husband to rest and to match my son's chipper energy, I whispered to him, "Let's go on a secret dawn Paw Patrol mission." (Yep, you caught that. The sun hadn't gotten out of bed yet either.)

You may or may not have entered the magical *Paw Patrol* phase yet, so let me quickly educate you. It's a television show about a team of pups who come to the rescue of their neighbors and friends in times of need or misfortune. Their human leader, Ryder, supplies them with all sorts of super vehicles, super costumes, and lots of tasty treats. My son is absolutely enamored with the *Paw Patrol* and will do just about anything to watch just one more episode (one more, puuuuleeeaaazzee).

Anyhow, that morning, when I told George that we would be going on a special Paw Patrol mission, his ears immediately perked up, he got very quiet, and whispered back, "Yes! Where are we going? Tell me everything!" I instructed him to quickly and quietly grab a pair of underwear and clothes from his dresser and hold my hand to gently tiptoe down the stairs. Once we arrived at the landing, I told him that I was going to sneak into the laundry room and throw on a cozy "costume" (which of course ended up being black leggings, UGG boots, and an oversized black jacket). I told him that for our secret mission, we were going to pick up some eggs, bacon, and cottage cheese for Daddy and surprise his Paw Patrol pups with a special treat for them (a.k.a., him): donuts!

His face lit up and he could barely contain his excitement. All the lights in the house remained off. I turned off the alarm and put up my pointer finger with a "shhh," and we snuck into Daddy's car to make our way to the closest grocery store.

Yes, all I did was get my ass out of bed and drive us to the grocery store at the crack of dawn, but to George, the entire experience dazzled him. He still talks about our secret Paw Patrol donut mission and asks when the next time is that we'll be getting an assignment from Ryder.

. . .

There are so many chores and must-do activities in our daily lives that are mundane, but they don't have to be. Most of us spend a lot of time doing laundry, dishes, cooking, cleaning, and grocery shopping . . . in addition to having careers. Although I would never categorize any one of those tasks as pleasurable, you can make them a bit more enjoyable. I'm sure you think that's ridiculous, but I promise it's not. The next time you need to do the laundry, let your child build a fort with your XL bed sheets. The next time you see the dishes piling up, crank up some Top 40 hits and time yourself to see how fast you can get them done. The next time you have to cook (when you really aren't feeling in the mood), let your child take the lead. Let them rinse the veggies, set the table, or program the oven. Jonelle from California says, "I love having music on while we do chores! We sing the 'Clean Up' song and dance around the house."

Finishing all the items on your to-do list can feel daunting (and stressful), but it doesn't have to. If you can get a bit more creative in your perception of these responsibilities and daily activities, you might appreciate the act of doing them.

No, you obviously won't do this *all* the time and, of course, there will be times when you'd just rather avoid errands and chores altogether, but it is worth trying to make them more fun (because there will always be things that must get accomplished). So let me give you a few ideas for things I do to make my errands and chores more entertaining:

- Add an element of mystery or intrigue (for example, the Paw Patrol mission I created above).
- Put on upbeat music, an uplifting podcast, or your favorite television show to distract you from any physical work you don't enjoy doing.
- Call up a friend or family member who you haven't spoken to in a while and catch up.
- Make yourself a treat to enjoy while you're doing your chores (coffee, tea, or a mocktail, anyone?).

- Involve your child (so that they learn to do whatever you're doing themselves and become much-needed helpers and more autonomous children).
- Turn a chore into a fun game (I Spy, Who can do X the fastest, and so on).

When you take the time to reframe your everyday routines into fast and fun play, I think you'll slowly discover that certain chores and errands aren't really *that* bad. They can surprisingly create some of the most memorable and satisfying experiences you have with your children. Since so much time is spent at home doing these sorts of activities, you might as well make the best of your time, don't you think?

You can also apply this concept to other daily routines that aren't necessarily "chores." For example, switching on the *Daniel Tiger* potty-training song when you can tell your child needs to pee, adopting a silly voice for one of your child's stuffed animals to use when it's time for them to brush their teeth, or pretending to be a superhero when your child is afraid of the "monsters" under their bed. Adding an element of humor and delight to almost any mundane activity will always have a better outcome.

Not the silly type? That's okay. You can often brighten daily activities just by brightening up your physical space. Hang some of your child's artwork on the entryway wall. Switch out your black dry-erase markers for some colorful ones. Buy a lime-green laundry basket or hot-pink oven mitts. It's amazing how the little things can make a big difference.

Journal Reflection

What do you think about the concept of reinventing your daily chores and routines? How might you make your everyday activities a bit more fun? Is there one chore you absolutely despise doing that you could delegate to your child? Do you think you might find more joy in your everyday life if you attempted to enjoy the chores you have to complete?

Exercise
DON'T BE COY, FIND THAT JOY

Materials: Your To-Do List
Time Commitment: As often as possible
Budget: Determined by you

In this exercise, commit to making at least one of daily chores or errands a bit more fun as often as possible. This may mean subscribing to an exciting and salacious podcast to listen to while you do the dishes or trying that crazy, over-the-top, new Starbucks concoction you've been eyeing while picking up groceries. It may also mean investing in some kid-friendly cooking utensils to gain a bit more help with daily meal prep. Chores can be fun if you allow them to be. I thoroughly enjoy watching my son dance to "Alejandro" by Lady Gaga on the couch while I fold our laundry.

FOLLOW-UP QUESTIONS

Which chore did you choose to enhance? Are you dreading that chore as much? Does it make sense to take on the challenge of making your other chores more fun as well? How do you think making your chores more fun might affect your usual mood or demeanor?

> *Tice Advice:*
> FINDING JOY IN THE MOST
> MUNDANE PLACES CAN ALSO
> BE THE MOST REWARDING,
> ENRICHING, AND MEMORABLE.

"The art of being happy lies in the power of extracting happiness from common things."

Henry Ward Beecher

Chapter 16
IT'S TIME TO
HAVE AN AFFAIR

How to Utilize Your Past
to Enrich Your Future

"If we listened to our intellect, we'd never have
a love affair. We'd never have a friendship.
We'd never go into business, because we'd
be cynical. . . . Well, that's nonsense. You've
got to jump off cliffs all the time and
build your wings on the way down."

Ray Bradbury

Growing up, I was always a determined and driven student. I studied diligently, followed the rules, showed
up to class on time, and maintained a 4.0 GPA. I always
prioritized studying and turned down invitations to parties
where I thought there might be "inappropriate behavior."
I was a nerd. I was awkward. I was *that* girl. The goodie
two shoes.

My determination in high school paid off when I was admitted to the University of Chicago (U of C) in 2002 (where, I might add, they pride themselves on their slogan, "Where fun comes to die"). U of C was a nose-to-the-grindstone, "let's get to work" sort of environment where students were fervently focused on learning. It was the perfect socially safe, nerdy culture that I felt I needed and craved. But, after the first month of school, I felt like somewhat of a fraud. Yes, I loved to learn, but I had to work extremely hard to keep up "intellectual appearances." What did I think of Nietzsche's works? What did I think a postapocalyptic world might look like, and what would be my plan for navigating it? Heck, if only I knew the answers to either of these questions.

Most of the students at U of C were what I would consider genius-level intellectuals, and I was just a mere commoner among them. Even though I enjoyed my schoolwork, I was also very interested in a few relatively superficial things, like makeup, fashion, the entertainment industry, going to fraternity parties, and being desired by men. I wanted an intellectual college experience, but I also craved a more stereotypical one.

Fast forward to my sophomore year. I was bumping along, getting decent grades, but feeling utterly lost in my quest for uncovering what I wanted to do with my life. I'd had an internship the previous summer at the University of Hawaii Department of Genetics Counseling and Mapping, only to discover that that line of work was not the right fit for me. So then the question became, now what? What was next?

My mom came to visit me on spring break and sat down to have a serious talk with me. We chatted at length about possible career paths (my parents always assumed I'd follow in the family footsteps and become a doctor) and my personal goals. As usual, we talked in circles and hypotheticals (getting nowhere fast), until my mom looked me directly in the eye and said, "Okay, cut the crap. What do you actually like doing? I don't care if it sounds ridiculous or for that matter, dumb. Just be honest." I took a deep breath, collected my thoughts, and embarrassingly said, "I like watching TV." Much to my surprise, my mom said, "Great! Time to work on finding you a job in television!"

It had never even crossed my mind that I could land a job in television, nor did I have a clue about where to start. But I learned in that moment that I had been having a love affair with television for years. I snuck out of bed late at night to watch my favorite programs. I recorded entire seasons of shows and labeled them with falsified titles so no one could judge my taste. I spent hours and hours being infatuated with and thinking about certain characters on my beloved programs. I fell in love with watching characters succeed, suffer, and triumph all while learning about different aspects of the human condition. I was deeply in love with television, but never in my wildest dreams did I believe I could turn my love affair into a viable career. But guess what? I did. I landed internships and jobs at local news and national stations, from MSNBC to MTV, and I worked in production as well as on camera.

I graduated from college with a job as a news anchor waiting for me. I had made my affair public and by choosing not to care about what anyone else thought, I found personal freedom and success. (And *pssst*. Love affairs can end or even ignite new sparks in different directions. Case in point, I broke up with television and began a new love affair with modeling only a few short years later.)

. . .

When was the last time you felt crazy energized and full of life? Do you remember what sparked that illustrious excitement? Well, it's time to take a trip down memory lane and revisit those moments. It's time to have a love affair . . . with yourself. It's incredibly easy to sleepwalk through daily routines and forget about the moments that helped define who you are today and who you want to be.

Yes, keeping and having routines when you have children is extremely important, but let's not forget *your* needs are equally important. When you feel undeniably alive, you project positivity and light into the universe and onto your kids. Isn't that worth fighting for? In my opinion, it's a win-win.

So, let's first break down what a love affair really is and, second, help you to begin one.

Love affair (*noun*): "an intense enthusiasm or liking for something."[38]

---

38. Lexico.com, "love affair (noun)," powered by Oxford, accessed on August 10, 2021, https://www.lexico.com/en/definition/love_affair.

Sounds about right, doesn't it? Who better to have a love affair with than yourself?

Now, let's consider societal connotations. When someone mentions that they are having an affair, typically it has a negative stigma associated with it. Most people immediately associate it with unhealthy infatuation, sneakiness, danger, or the like. But isn't the definition itself all about having an "intense enthusiasm and liking" for something or someone? Shouldn't that inherently be a *good* thing? For whatever reason, most of us have been taught that having intensely positive experiences or feelings should make us feel guilty or ashamed . . . that we should keep these feelings to ourselves and hide them. But why?

The ebbs and flows in our emotions are what make us interesting and unique. When you are willing and open to having a love affair with yourself, it's amazing how your personal narrative can shift and help you to define your true desires.

The next question becomes, how do you start one and what does it look like? From my experience, a love affair can come in a variety of forms that may feel selfish (but are not), yet they feel exhilarating and rejuvenating.

Let me give you a few examples of types of love affairs that I feel are extremely beneficial:

1. FALLING IN LOVE WITH YOUR APPEARANCE AGAIN.

This might mean experimenting with clothes or makeup that are out of your comfort zone or spending some time at the gym to tone your body. These are worthy goals because, guess what? When you look your best, you often feel your best. Yes, I know it sounds shallow, but it's true. Think about it. Do you feel better when you've just had a blow out at a salon or when your hair is frizzy and out of control? Do you feel better lying in bed in your pajamas or wearing a power suit to run your errands? Just putting an extra ten minutes a day into improving your image can have substantial benefits. As the adage goes, "Dress for the job you want, not the one you have."

When you have this kind of affair, give yourself permission to indulge a bit. Isn't that what an affair is all about? Buy that lipstick or pair of jeans that's out of your budget every once in awhile. Kathleen from Illinois loves running outside until she gets a "runner's high" (a.k.a., mental clarity). Do that juice cleanse you've been putting off. Take a bubble bath in the middle of the day. You get it. Taking care of yourself in this way shouldn't be considered vain; it should be praised. I'm giving you permission to focus on yourself so that you can put your best foot forward to the world. You might even be surprised by the response you get. The universe knows when you feel good and typically rewards you for sending out those extra positive vibes. When you put in the time to love yourself, you attract like-minded and inspiring people (at least that's always been the case for me).

2. HAVE AN AFFAIR WITH AN OLD PASSION.

When you think about your past, can you think of something you fell in love with (that wasn't required of you)? I'm talking about finger painting, horseback riding, pottery, playing the piano, making macaroni jewelry, and so on. This "something" could be totally silly, but you remember it as truly *fun*. I'm not talking about something you did when you were bored, but rather something that made you feel inspired. This type of affair is for you to reconnect with your inner child and get back to basics.

What could this look like? Maybe it means you taking out your child's play dough and making your own figurines. Booking yourself a guitar lesson. Writing a short story or making a documentary film with your smartphone. Maybe it's reading comic books or baking your favorite cookies. Having this type of affair is all about indulging in the activities that make you happy. Put everyone else's opinions aside and do what feeds your soul.

At first it may feel a bit awkward since it's probably been quite some time since you revisited this special something, but just like rekindling beloved relationships, there is something beautifully comforting and alluring about it. Don't let that get away from you. Snatch it up. You are in control of this affair, and you have the power to decide when you want it to begin as well as end. And don't forget, you are allowed to have as many of these affairs as you'd like. No need to choose just one. Have multiple.

3. HAVE AN AFFAIR WITH A NEW DREAM.

As much as I love having affairs with old passions, I also love having affairs with novel lifestyles and vocations. One of the most wonderful parts of being human is that our goals and dreams are fluid—always changing and transforming. One day we want X and the next we want Y. That's okay. That's perfectly normal and essential to leading a more fulfilling life. We must dream new dreams in order to challenge and demolish the walls which we build for ourselves. When you have an affair with a new dream, you spend time daydreaming about what ifs. Then, when you pin down what it is that you are truly projecting in these daydreams, you *must* chase it. Having the daydreams themselves are a good catalyst for change, but once you make the first move toward achieving your dream, you might be pleasantly surprised by the outcome. Beth from Massachusetts said that she only discovered how much she loved event planning after becoming a "room mom" and putting together special events for her child's classroom. She now loves spending her free time throwing fundraisers and parties for her child's school. "I didn't know how much I loved party planning until I randomly volunteered one afternoon."

(**Side note**: Give yourself time in this process. Please don't put pressure on yourself to come up with some elaborate exotic dream that really isn't your own. Be kind to yourself. It's perfectly acceptable to take baby steps. For example, it may be easier for you to wrap your head around the idea of creating your own shop of handmade goods on Etsy rather than opening a boutique in Paris. Think about it this way: you must lay the foundation on a house before you even consider building a second story.)

Journal Reflection

How do you feel about the idea of starting a love affair? Did you feel motivated or overwhelmed? How do you think you might benefit from having one or more of these affairs? Was there anything that immediately came to mind when you thought of having a love affair with a new dream or an old one? If so, describe them.

Exercise
Start a Love Affair Now

Materials: Determined by you
Time Commitment: 5–10 minutes daily, for at least a week
Budget: Dependent on which type of love affair you choose

I'm sure you saw this coming, but in this exercise, I'm asking you to start at least one love affair *today*. Take just five minutes right now. Close your eyes and allow yourself to daydream about the type of love affairs you might like to have. You can choose as many or as few as you'd like. Do you want to learn how to scuba dive? Do you wish you could open a restaurant in your favorite neighborhood? Do you think it might be fun to play dress up with your child? Or dye your hair black or blonde? From appearance to matters of the heart and soul, the possibilities are endless. You just have to start. Put aside any fear you may have, because *I know you've got this.*

FOLLOW-UP QUESTIONS

Describe the love affair you chose to begin. How has it made you feel? What is the most significant thing this love affair has done for you at this point? Has it improved your ego or your focus? How long would you like this love affair to go on? Are you willing or able to start another one simultaneously? If so, describe what it is and go for it.

Tice Advice:
HAVING ONE OR MORE LOVE AFFAIRS
WITH YOURSELF IS ESSENTIAL
TO ENRICHING YOUR LIFE.

"Deep in your wounds are seeds,
waiting to grow beautiful flowers."

Niti Majethia

Chapter 17

TRUST ISN'T EASY, BUT IT IS WORTH IT

WHY TRUSTING YOUR INTUITION IS ESSENTIAL

"All the world is made of faith,
and trust, and pixie dust."

J. M. Barrie, Peter Pan

When I had George, I had just turned thirty-three years old. I was already getting "long in the tooth" as a model by industry standards and was unsure if my career would be waiting for me after I gave birth. I spent quite a lot of time worrying about if I'd get my body back to where it needed to be or if my hiatus away from work would be held against me. I also wondered if my agency would continue to represent me, since it was one of the most reputable agencies in the world.

On top of that, leaving New York and moving to California and then Texas didn't do me any favors workwise because it required more travel and expense, not only for me but also for my clients. I was also fiercely attached to George postpartum and refused to leave him overnight during the first eighteen months of his life. In my mind, I had undone over ten years of hard work in less than two years. I had inadvertently rendered my personal brand passé by prioritizing my son.

Then, when I thought I *might* be ready to restart my modeling career, I felt insecure and anxious. How would my clients feel now that I was a mom? Would the clients I had before still view me in the same way? Would my agency choose to release me or attempt to rebrand and remarket me? Would they ask me to lose or gain weight? Cut my hair or mandate a style change?

Truth was, I had lost confidence in myself because I was unsure of my true goals and priorities now that George had become a permanent fixture in my life. Without fully understanding my feelings, I attempted to dip my foot back into the fashion world without the same fervent passion I once possessed. I wanted to help provide for my family, but I wasn't ready or willing to put in the necessary effort to make it in such a cutthroat business. Due to my self-doubt and deflated ego, I wasn't surprised when my agency released me.

Was my career over? Was this the end? Did I really want to say goodbye to a job that provided me with so much joy and happiness? A job that allowed me to travel all over the world and meet extremely inspiring and creative people? A job that made me feel so beautiful (inside and out)?

After I was dropped from the agency, I agonized over these questions for over two years. If I wasn't going to be a model, what was I going to be? What else did I really enjoy? Then, it hit me. I didn't want to be anything else. I loved being a curve model. I wanted to model again. I looked in the mirror and thought to myself, "I don't care what anyone else thinks. If this is my passion, nothing is going to stop me." I began to trust myself again. I listened to my gut and my instincts. I regained my sense of confidence and decided to hit the ground running. I knew that the right agent at the right agency would see my worth and value having me as a part of their team.

So I booked myself a trip to New York and set up as many meetings as I could with a slew of major agencies. I trusted that the universe understood and felt my intentions and would reward me accordingly. I wasn't wrong. Sure, I got rejected by more than few agencies, but I got the one *yes* that I *really* wanted, from ONE Management. My ten years of hard work hadn't been for nothing. Two of the agents I had loved working with at my previous agency had moved over to ONE and were excited to represent me once again (stretch marks, rolls, and all).

At thirty-seven, here I was signing a new modeling contract with one of the most prestigious agencies in New York. I was signing not as a gorgeous teen or a stunning sophomore in college, but as a self-aware, sophisticated, and mature mom . . . and it wasn't long before I was shooting with some of the biggest names in the business once again. (Curious about how my modeling career has progressed? Go find me on Instagram @amandatice and see for yourself.)

. . .

I can't help but give my mom credit for my relentless quest to succeed and live a fuller life. My mom has always been a wonderful role model by consistently trusting herself and never shying away from her interests. When she decided that she had grown tired of practicing dentistry and wanted to make more time for me, she quit. She quickly realized how much she loved finance, and the next thing I knew, she had glued herself to CNBC to learn everything she could about stocks and investing. Because she loved it so much and trusted in her own abilities, she became a successful day trader within mere months . . . and within a few years, she had made enough money for our entire family to have the luxury of moving to Hawaii and living on the beach! It is really all about trusting and having faith in yourself.

Raise your hand if you have a little voice in your head that perpetuates fear and worry! You know, the voice that tells you that you're going to make a mistake, that you won't be successful, that you can't do X, Y, or Z because of excuse numbers one, two, or three? Yep, this little voice haunts me too and she's a real bitch. I don't just dislike her; I hate her. At times, she keeps me from trying new things, improving my life, and being my best self. She is insanely good at bringing me down and keeping me down if I allow her to.

Whether I like it or not, she's not going anywhere. It's up to me to tame her, while also realizing her value and worth. Although she's a complete bitch, she exists for a reason. She is your primal voice, the one who would have protected you from dangerous predators and life-threatening situations in centuries past. She is the biological equivalent of your internal safety net—the voice whose only true motivation is survival. She doesn't care about your hopes and dreams. All she cares about is that you make easy, simple decisions that ensure you are alive, sheltered, well-fed, and breathing. She doesn't care about your ego and, in fact, despises it. To her, it's gratuitous. But she is the one you must befriend and love. After all, she believes she has your best interests at heart.

Although she will always be a permanent fixture in your brain, surprisingly, she can also be reasoned with. With time and practice, you may even change her narrative or at least soften it. If you remain open-minded, you may make her work for *you* . . . and I'm going to tell you how to do it.

STEP ONE: GET VERY QUIET AND LISTEN

The first and hardest thing you have to do is start listening to her. Instead of shoving her opinions down into the depths of your psyche and plowing forward, you must hear her out. Over the course of your life, you consciously and subconsciously assimilate certain narratives about yourself, some of which are true and some of which are false. Until you understand why you've assimilated certain beliefs and determined which ones are serving you, you will never achieve any sort of freedom—and you will continue to be stifled by her. But, if you take the time and do the hard work, you may realize that she has the potential to become your greatest motivator.

TRY THIS EXERCISE

When she starts going off about how you aren't qualified for a job, promotion, or financial success, ask her why and see what she has to say. Write down her excuses in your journal. Then, you must determine which of those excuses hold truth and which are ridiculous. Then, ask yourself, "What's the absolute worst that could happen if I pursue this opportunity?"

This where you have to get really honest with yourself and leave no stone unturned. Is your fear failure? What happens if you do fail? Will you starve and face homelessness? Will the people you love stop caring about you? Will your parents disown you? Will it embarrass your children? Will your friends think less of you? (Be sure to record all the answers to these questions.)

Then, change the framing and ask yourself, "What's the absolute best thing that could happen if I pursue this opportunity?" What if you put yourself out there and you succeed? You gain recognition and fortune? You improve your financial independence or provide a better life for yourself as well as your loved ones? You have a job that you genuinely love? Isn't that worth the risk?

Sure, none of it is easy, but wouldn't you feel proud of yourself that you put yourself out there and you tried? That you proved to yourself that you could overcome your fears?

Let me tell you—that's admirable to *everyone*. So, why hold onto any negative beliefs that are impeding your success? Sure, grappling with these insecurities isn't any fun, but the reality is, *you are the one who built the wall that's holding you back and only you have the demolition equipment to destroy it.* So, look back at your list and consciously strike through the false beliefs with a black marker, giving them a big "Screw You."

STEP TWO: RECALIBRATE YOUR MENTAL FRAMING

Once you've forced your fears into the front of your mind and placed them under a brightly lit microscope, then you can really get into the dirty work of retooling and reframing all of the useless untrue beliefs you hold about yourself. Recalibrating how you frame your thoughts takes time and practice, but it can be amazingly beneficial. Once you acknowledge that these negative thoughts and behaviors both exist and are directly impacting your ability to succeed, they somehow become much easier to control and tame. You now have the ability to regain power and sit in the driver's seat.

TRY THIS EXERCISE

Take a few minutes to play a game I like to call, "Active Annie." Who is Active Annie? She's your new go-to BFF, spiritual cheerleader, and the voice of optimism and reason.

She is the immortal enemy of your negative voice, Debbie Downer. Active Annie is the one whom you need to call upon when you notice self-doubt creeping back into your thoughts. Here's how she works:

> Debbie Downer says, "I'm shy, boring, and overweight. No one will ever hire me for a sales job where I'm the face of the company."
>
> Active Annie, on the other hand says, "Excuse me, but I'm not sure who you're referring to. I'm vibrant, bright, and motivated. Any company would be lucky to employ me. It's time for me to get out there and submit that application I've been holding onto for weeks!"
>
> Debbie Downer has every intention of playing it safe for all the wrong reasons. She hasn't done her research. She is a coward. Active Annie, on the other hand, knows your strengths and knows that this opportunity may have the ability to improve your quality of life. Active Annie is ready to take steps in the right direction to ensure forward mobility with your permission.

Now that you know how Active Annie and Debbie Downer both speak to you, take the time to play their game. Conjure up one negative belief that you think is impeding your success or stifling your happiness in your personal or professional life. Then, grab your journal and write out a short dialogue between these two voices. Who do you think is more reasonable? Who do you think can improve your life? I'm going to go out on a limb here and say . . . Active Annie. She is as much a part of you as Debbie Downer, and, boy, is she more fun to be around!

STEP THREE: WALK DOWN MEMORY LANE

It's no secret that women often tend to undervalue themselves as well as downplay their strengths and successes. Instead of focusing on their worth, they often focus on what they don't possess instead of what they do. Why is that? Because for decades, society has told us we're not good enough, just like I highlighted in chapter five. This is BS! It's time for an internal revolution. It's time to reprogram these faulty codes and remember why we're so awesome. All we need to do is retrace our steps and find our way back to this important conclusion. It's time to tap into the belief systems that we explored in steps one and two. How?

TRY THIS EXERCISE

Get out your journal and get ready to answer a lot of feel-good questions (because, Mama, you deserve this). Answer each of these questions honestly and thoughtfully; and don't be shy, be **BOLD**:

1. What are some of your greatest accomplishments to date? How did you achieve said accomplishments? What do these accomplishments say about your strengths?

2. What are you the proudest of, personally and professionally?

3. Remind yourself of a time when you handled a difficult situation beautifully. What exactly did you do or say? How did it make you feel afterward?

4. What has been the best job you've ever had and why? Why do you think the employer hired you (or you independently excelled)?

5. When was a time where you felt extremely valued and appreciated? What did you do or say to receive that praise?

6. What would your best friends say is your most admirable quality and why? What about your partner or your child—what would they say?

7. What kind of legacy would you like to leave?

Now, take a few minutes and reflect on the answers you wrote to these questions. Reread them. Then, answer one more question, "Can you see your worth now?" Because, let me tell you, I can. I see you. I know that you are resilient and strong even though I don't personally know you. I know that because you took the time to answer these questions, you really care about improving your life and the lives of others. Each one of us is gifted in our own special way, and I know that the universe wants you to share your gift, whatever it may be. All you have to do is tap into it, take a leap of faith, and *trust yourself*. You've got this. I know you do.

Your Final Exercise
THE LOVE JAR

Materials: Jar with lid, brightly colored paper, pen, scissors (optional but recommended: individually wrapped pieces of dark chocolate)

Time Commitment: 30–45 minutes

Budget: $15

As much as I'd like to believe that I have the ability to live in a constant self-trustworthy mind state, I know that's unrealistic. Debbie Downer ensures that my worries and insecurities will never fully be at bay, which is why I created this easy and uplifting exercise to provide the reminders you may need to activate and reinstall Active Annie at any time.

In this exercise, I am going to ask you to finish the sentences that I have provided for you. Take the time to write out each entire sentence on a few different pieces of colored paper. Then, use your scissors to cut these sentences into strips and fold them over. Once done, place all your folded sentence strips into your jar (along with the pieces of chocolate you hopefully purchased).

Voila! Now you have yourself an awesome self-love jar! Whenever you need a pick-me-up, or a friendly reminder as to why you should never doubt yourself, you have a physical object you can quickly open and reference with kick-ass answers. Being able to reflect on your strengths at a moment's notice or during a difficult time can spark an immediate positive shift in mood and perception. This jar should not be hidden; in fact it should be visible to you regularly. Without even having to open it, it should remind you of all the reasons why you rock.

SENTENCE PROMPTS

I have included my personal answers to these sentence prompts in order to help guide you to discovering yours.

1. The thing I admire the most about myself is . . .
   (that I often thrive in the face of change).
2. I am worthy of love because . . .
   (I give love unconditionally).
3. It makes me so happy . . .
   (to have such a wonderful family).
4. I am so good at . . .
   (recognizing other people's strengths).
5. I love the fact that I am . . .
   (nerdy, transparent, silly, and thoughtful).
6. I believe my friends love me because . . .
   (I'm honest, open, and a little bit wacky).
7. If I could be anything, I would be . . .
   (an inspirational coach to as many moms
   as possible).
8. I'm so lucky because . . .
   (I have an amazing family, thoughtful friends,
   and a career I love).
9. What makes me unique is that . . .
   (I'm typically not afraid to try new things).

10. I'm proud to take some time to focus on myself because . . .

    (I can't be a role model for my son if I don't know who I am or who I want to be).

11. The most important thing I need to remind myself is . . .

    (that I am needed and loved).

12. Life sure isn't easy, but . . .

    (it sure can be a lot of fun!).

13. If I were granted one wish, it would be . . .

    (that everyone I loved [including myself] could live long, prosperous, healthy, and happy lives).

14. I am proud of myself . . .

    (for writing this book and believing I could do it).

15. I refuse to have any regrets because I believe . . .

    (every aspect of life has the ability to be a lesson, which promotes personal growth).

Tice Advice:
WHEN YOU ARE TRUE TO YOURSELF
AND TRUST YOUR INSTINCTS, YOU
GAIN THE POWER TO UNLEASH
YOUR GREATEST POTENTIAL.

"The hardest step she ever took was to blindly trust in who she was."

Atticus

Final Journal Reflection

At the end of the day, I strongly believe that all anyone truly wants is to be loved and feel like their life has had purpose. Without knowing you, I can already tell you that your life has meaning and will continue to be meaningful, for you mean the world to your child and they wouldn't be here if it weren't for you. As long as your belly is full, there's a roof over your head, and your children are safe and healthy, be abundantly grateful. Whatever bump in the road you've hit, you *will* get over it. All you need is to believe and trust in yourself. You *will* persevere. Constance Tice, my fabulous mother, also gave me the best advice I can think of, "The happier of a person you are, the happier your child will be."

So, tell me, what has this book and the exercises included within it taught you about yourself? Have you made any strides or improvements in your overall happiness? Do you now see why you have the ability to take over the world, dream a new dream, or ignite an old passion? Do you now fully understand just how much is constantly being asked of you and just how well you're coping with all of it? Are you finally seizing your life and showing it who is boss? I hope so, because you are a force to be reckoned with and an inspiration to all. You are freaking *amazing*! Congrats on rewiring your new mom code!

See You Later

Hello again, fellow mama,

I sincerely hope that this book has given you the opportunity to redefine yourself as well as provide you with the tools needed to take on whatever challenges you face and await you. Navigating the bumpy waters of postpartum life is no cakewalk, but I have every confidence in you that you're now well equipped to live your best life and become the best version of yourself. Of course, change takes hard work, but I think we both know that the work is more than worth it. When you can see and feel the transformation in your household, mood, conduct, and daily routine, then you'll know that you've found your groove.

Although I've most likely never met you in person, I can almost guarantee that we are kindred spirits. We are both women, figuring out how to steer our ship, *The Motherhood*, on its maiden voyage, and doing anything and everything we can to make sure that our vessel stays afloat and arrives safely to our desired destination. We may not be from the same economic or racial background, but we are both part of the same exclusive VIP club: The Moms Club, rewriting the new mom code. I've got your back, and I know you've got mine. So, if you see me at the park, at a coffee shop, on an airplane, or even in a Target bathroom (with those damn auto-flushing toilets that toddlers love!), please say hello. It's true that when you find your tribe, you find your vibe; and the larger your tribe, the greater the potential for exponential growth, joy, and enrichment. So, cheers, Mama. Let's raise a glass (of La Croix) and toast to the new you, the new me, and the wild ride that is and will continue to be motherhood!

"The light within me chooses to honor the light within you." Namaste, Mama!

With love, Amanda

About the Author

AMANDA TICE is a successful curve model, former TV journalist, and proud mom to George. She is passionate about helping other new mothers not only reach their full potential but also feel less alone in their journey through motherhood.

She is currently represented by major modeling agencies worldwide and has built a strong client base over the past twelve years, working for and with dozens of retail clients such as Nordstrom, Target, Saks, and Kohl's. Amanda is also a versatile and dynamic entrepreneur with experience in branding and events. As the founder of Hatch Studios (a former coworking space in LA), she excels in community building and generating creative strategies for success. She secured sponsorships from top brands including ZICO and American Airlines while there.

Amanda was also on-camera talent for MSNBC, MTV, and Plum TV. Throughout her television career, she spent her time interviewing A-list celebrities and designers, covering large events like Milan and NY Fashion Week, and producing segments for a variety of media outlets.

Amanda received an honors bachelor's degree in comparative human development from the University of Chicago. She lives in Austin with her husband and their son.

I WOULD APPRECIATE YOUR FEEDBACK
ON WHAT CHAPTERS HELPED YOU MOST
AND WHAT YOU WOULD LIKE TO
SEE IN FUTURE BOOKS.

IF YOU ENJOYED THIS BOOK AND
FOUND IT HELPFUL, PLEASE
LEAVE A **REVIEW** ON AMAZON.

VISIT ME AT

WWW.AMANDATICE.COM

WHERE YOU CAN SIGN UP
FOR EMAIL UPDATES.

Thank You!